Performing Purity

Critical Intercultural Communication Studies

Thomas K. Nakayama
General Editor

Vol. 6

PETER LANG
New York • Washington, D.C./Baltimore • Bern
Frankfurt am Main • Berlin • Brussels • Vienna • Oxford

John T. Warren

Performing Purity

Whiteness, Pedagogy,
and the Reconstitution of Power

PETER LANG
New York • Washington, D.C./Baltimore • Bern
Frankfurt am Main • Berlin • Brussels • Vienna • Oxford

Library of Congress Cataloging-in-Publication Data

Warren, John T.
Performing purity: whiteness, pedagogy,
and the reconstitution of power / John T. Warren.
p. cm. — (Critical intercultural communication studies; v. 6)
Includes bibliographical references and index.
1. Whites—Race identity—United States. 2. Whites—Study and teaching—United
States. 3. Identity (Psychology)—United States. 4. Performative (Philosophy).
5. Performing arts—Social aspects—United States. 6. Purity, Ritual—United States.
7. Purity (Philosophy). 8. Power (Social sciences)—United States. 9. United States—
Race relations. 10. United States—Race relations—Study and teaching.
I. Title. II. Series.
E184.A1W255   305.8'034073—dc21   2003040066
ISBN 0-8204-6754-5
ISSN 1528-6118

Bibliographic information published by **Die Deutsche Bibliothek**.
Die Deutsche Bibliothek lists this publication in the "Deutsche
Nationalbibliografie"; detailed bibliographic data is available
on the Internet at http://dnb.ddb.de/.

Cover design by Dutton & Sherman Design

The paper in this book meets the guidelines for permanence and durability
of the Committee on Production Guidelines for Book Longevity
of the Council of Library Resources.

Special thanks to ...

Renee, Schuyler, and Lucy and their students, who made this project possible.

My advisors from Southern Illinois University-Carbondale.

My colleagues at Bowling Green State University.

Keith, Amy, Deanna, Kathy, & John.

My family.

Gina.

Table of Contents

Acknowledgments

There are two kinds of people in this world: those who like acknowledgments and those who find them frustratingly icky. I like them. If you are one of those who fall on the icky side, please turn rapidly to the next page. If you want to hear sweet things about some of the people I love most, please join me in celebrating their contributions to this book.

First, I would like to extend my thanks to the teachers who offered up their classrooms for my ethnographic eyes. It is a huge risk to permit a researcher access to your teaching and your students. Renee, Schuyler, and Lucy graciously allowed me access to themselves and their students. I extend my most heartfelt thanks to these outstanding teachers, as well as the generous students who also granted me permission to observe. It was a gift. These pages are my attempt to make that gift matter.

This book could not have been completed without the generous contribution of two scholarly communities. First, the speech communication community at Southern Illinois University-Carbondale shaped and gave life to this project. Elyse Pineau, Craig Gingrich-Philbrook, Lenore Langsdorf, Ron Pelias, Jennifer Willis-Rivera, Jonny Gray, and others have given me strength and focus. Amy Kilgard, Keith Nainby, John Pea, Deanna Fassett, Marcyrose Chvasta, Carleen Spry, Jill Hildebrandt, Keith Berry, Kristen Treinen, Bryant Alexander, and the rest of my colleagues from SIUC have given me the love and support I needed to survive in Carbondale. Special thanks to Kathy Hytten, who surpassed all expectations of friendship. When I think back to who I am as a scholar today, it is primarily because of Kathy's critical eye and warm words. Second, the community of Bowling Green State University. The colleagues and friends I have found here encouraged me to be better, to do more. The Department of Interpersonal Communication/School of Communication Studies faculty, thank you for welcoming me to my new home. Specifically, thanks to my lunch bunch: Lynda Dee Dixon, Paige Edley, Radhika Gajjala, Laura Lengel, and Denise Menchaca. Also, thanks to Vivian Patraka and the Institute for Culture and Society Writing Group, each of whom kept pushing me to "honor the work." Also, my thanks to Christine Pease-Hernandez and

Amy Heuman who served as my research assistants the past two years. Christine's early work getting me going and Amy's work getting me to the finish line has made all the difference. Additionally, this project would not have been possible without the support and care from my Fall 2002 COMS 640 course—the men and women in that course were patient during an otherwise crazy semester. And my continued thanks to Tom Nakayama and the folks at Peter Lang for seeing this work to print.

Finally, I would like to thank my family. From my brothers to my aunts and uncles, my family may not totally understand what I do, but they are supportive of my voyage. In particular, thanks to my parents for never swaying in their support of my ambitions. The love they have given me is truly a gift I treasure. Thanks to my brothers, my nephews, my niece, and my extended family everywhere for so many years of love and encouragement. And, especially, my thanks to Gina DeRosa Warren—I am always grateful to have such a wonderful companion. Thanks for being there for me.

John Pea always says that in everything he does, he hears the voices of those who has meant so much to him echoing in his head. With that said, if you hear something in this document that sounds like you . . . it probably is.

Introduction

A Preliminary Peek at the Machine

I am sitting at a conference, suffering from "hotel-back"—you know, that stiff back that comes from too many nights in pseudo-elegant beds, long sessions sitting in poorly shaped hotel chairs, and caffeine-enhanced presentation anxiety. I am listening this time, watching a session featuring a colleague, a friend of mine. I bend over to pick up my program to see how many more papers are left on the panel, how many more minutes of this before the next stretch, how many more. I feel the vinyl lining of my briefcase against the back of my hand as I search for my program when I hear her say it. My head pops up and I take in her words, her body. I see her hands slightly shake as she reads, evidence of an inexperienced presenter (I think this knowing that mine shake as well), and I glance at the others on the panel staring outward, unfazed. I feel as if I am the only one in motion, the only one seeing, the only one who knows, the only one. My head turns around, the audience is engaged with her talk, the other panelists are engaged, everyone is engaged. Everyone but me—I think this knowing that it's bound to be untrue but I can't shake this feeling—I can't shake this feeling that I am the only one. I look back at her and watch as she turns the page, placing the top sheet of bleached type-filled pages under the rest. A small gesture, a tapping of the pages on the desk and the pages are in order, neat and tidy. The irony of the moment strikes me and I want to laugh, but I don't.

*****

In cultural studies research focusing on whiteness, the body is a problem. Researchers studying race have long either relied on the body's physicality as the beginning of research or discounted the physical as a misleading remnant of modernity's essentialism trap; yet the problem of the body persists. The tensions between the physical body as a material representation of racial identity with particular social and political effects and the body as a rhetorical construct situated in social processes either leaves the physical body as the essentialized center of attention or completely erases the body. Both approaches, however, never really address the body in complex ways. The limitations in these research perspectives leave the real question in race studies unanswered, unasked: How can we locate the mechanisms in place that might illuminate a way of seeing How the body in general, and racial identity in particular, is constituted and reconstituted in everyday communicative interaction? In this project, I desire to develop a meaningful perspective for addressing this important question left unanswered in research on race and identity. I wish to offer a reading of people located in time and space that resists essentialism while understanding the rhetorical power of whiteness as a social construct by articulating an integrated approach to the body that looks at racial identity as an ongoing performative accomplishment.

*****

I replay that moment in my head, remembering what she had said: "The first school I went into was completely unorganized—the halls echoed with voices in a chaotic cacophony of noise while bodies moved from room to room ... and I knew that students couldn't possibly learn in this environment." I cringe again at the echo of that description, hearing another echo—this one from earlier in the paper, where she described this "chaotic" school: "Well, this school was predominantly of-color." I wonder if she understands the implications of what she just said. Again I look out and notice people taking notes. Perhaps they are writing what I am thinking; perhaps I am thinking what they are writing. My ears on alert, waiting to see if she would do it. I mean, the stage is set; the other school, the one more evenly populated with white and nonwhite students, would be next, but would she do it? I look around and no one else is noticing. I reach up and wipe my brow, now damp, as if the sweat could be stopped now, now that I feel the temperature in my body rise to match the dry hotel-heated room. I shift my body in the hard chair, trying to force comfort on my tired body. Then she says it, and I flinch.

"The second school was very different than the last. The halls were quiet, calm. They were clean—everything in its place. I could tell that learning was central here." The "civility" of her description is striking. The order of those halls, order described as quiet, absent of voice, absent of bodies, absent of those traits that contaminate, absent of that which messes it all up. I close my eyes and see an image of the two schools: The first stems from that cinematic school in Dead Poets' Society *(1990), with Robin Williams telling the privileged white boys to stand on their desks, thirty pairs of perfectly polished shoes on the smooth polished desktops. The other image also derives from Hollywood: In the film* 187 *(1997), where Samuel L. Jackson moves through a hallway filled with bodies, moving bodies, moving black bodies, and is grabbed, stabbed, and left to bleed against a graffiti-littered wall. I know that those images, brought forth by this scholar at this conference, are not accidental. These images are not in her paper; however, the paper is not really what is important—it's the pattern. It's the repetition of those images, those constructs, those descriptions. These descriptions are not absent ideology; they are ideological descriptions—descriptions born of an ideology of whiteness.*

*****

Lisa Delpit argues that institutions, specifically institutions of education, are predicated on the rules of the culture of power, which she implicitly names middle-class whiteness. Furthermore, she contends that people of color's success in these institutions depends on their ability to acquire the norms and behaviors "of the culture of those in power" (25). If one considers the typical enactment of "good student," the student who "learns" and "succeeds" in institutionally measurable ways in the education system, then one must also consider that those behaviors stem from a particular cultural location. These representations of the ideal, reified in schools across the country, of students quietly working at their desks, listening attentively, and raising their hands for permission to speak cannot be blindly accepted as a social norm if we are to understand where such representations of civility derive. The fact that students of color enter education and many times fail to know the codes of the culture of power and are then disproportionally placed in remedial tracks (Delpit) suggests the need to study the ways in which systems of whiteness either mutate or expel those bodies that cannot fit into mainstream educational practice. It is the goal of this study to consider how whiteness manifests in classrooms, in explicit and in subtle ways.

*****

The last bit of resistance holding back my headache gives way as the throbbing comes in swift and powerful bursts. I have to wait until the end of her paper, so I make deep marks on my tablet. I write: "I am amazed at a scholar invested in 'whiteness studies' who continues to reinscribe racism through her very language." I want to get out of here. I want to interrupt this, break in and make her see, make them all see, as if I have any of the answers, any of the answers they want to hear. When the papers cease, questions begin and I look around and see a well-respected Latina scholar who has come to witness our conversation, our white conversation. She raises her hand and, with the elegance of simplicity, offers a brief question to the panel: "Do white folks ever see or document how whiteness gets done? I mean, I see it but I wonder if you all do." Suddenly, I am hit with the force of her words. In my self-congratulatory thinking, sitting here seeing what no one else sees, this subtle example of white racism, I realize that only my own whiteness could create this illusion of singular awareness.

I look toward this scholar of color with hope, but then I notice it. Everyone is very quiet, taking notes on the back page of their program, looking out the window, glancing at their watches, or even just sitting there smiling and nodding. I look at myself, also seated, also writing, also relatively quiet except for the occasional sound of lead on paper. We are functioning so smoothly, so cleanly; we are so organized, so civil. I see something happening here, something I am not meant to see. Like an illusion with a minor flaw, I, for a moment, see the machinery—I see behind the curtain and notice that the wizard is nothing but a construction for our collective security.

*****

I have tried to address what happened in that conference several times. I remain unclear as to the best strategy to unfold the layers of that event, but I know that in some real ways I caught a glimpse of whiteness in the making. The crack in the illusion of whiteness allowed the whole mechanism to unfold in that moment: the panelists' posture, the mode of interaction, the turn-taking, the rows of seats, and the gentle questioning by the audience. I began to see, hear, and feel the practices of whiteness—to notice myself and others engaging in activities that carry its cultural power.

But, even as I saw it, it already began to blur. As I strained to take note of this experience, I felt my body again finding comfort in whiteness. As I looked toward these productions, these performances of whiteness, I realized how seductive the machinery of whiteness is for me as a white-constituted person. So easy was it to allow the film of my cultural power to obscure the making of my own privilege. So easy was it to slide back into the machine, another well-oiled joint in the production of power. Even when I resisted that desire, eventually I was able to allow it to continue to function. However, what remained in me was a desire to foster a new way of seeing whiteness in light of cultural production, to expose where bodily and discursive expressions constitute the white subject. This desire is at the heart of this work.

Karen: An Ethnographic Exemplar

When I began my ethnographic research, I knew, at a basic level, that I wanted to study race through the lens of the performative. I wanted to see race in the acts of production, through communicative repetition. However, I was not very certain how important this lens would become as I progressed. What seemed like a logical way of seeing whiteness took on new life as I entered the classroom. Suddenly, the literature I had read and that had informed my notions of race became more complicated. The literature often elided some differences in order to foreground others, creating static images of their participants. Who was white, who was not—these became easy categories, easy labels to rely on when the researcher entered the field. Yet, when I got to the classroom that was to be my ethnographic site for the next two years, I had a much harder time with these labels. Minor skips in the racialized tape caused me to rethink my assumptions. For instance, one student I had "naturally" assumed to be white was, in fact, of Middle Eastern descent. Other students looked nonwhite, but their "real" identities were much harder to discern. My efforts at comparing how students of different racial/ethnic backgrounds sat, talked, and moved through the classroom provided me with very little—there was not much to hold onto when the analysis was done. All I had was weak observations based on preestablished racial categories. In these ways, the labels I had grown to trust became relatively unhelpful in my efforts to see how students performed race.

In the end, I decided to focus on how race was discursively accomplished, rather than try to apply some ambiguous label to my participants. How do students talk about and create performances about race and difference in ways that work to reproduce inequities? This change meant that I could watch and learn from my participants, seeking to see the modes of production that are at work in the classroom. I could see students reconstituting race. For instance, consider the following example from my fieldnotes, in which Karen, an ethnographic participant, makes a "racist" comment.[1]

It all began when Renee, the instructor for the course, was taking attendance before the class period began. Karen and Diana sat next to each other, and Renee stood at the front of the room. Karen, a self-identified nontraditional white student, and another student were discussing the distance between campus and two nearby cities, trying to determine which location was a closer drive. Karen contended that both towns were of equal distance from the university, unless "construction or a traffic accident slowed you down." At some point in the conversation, Karen told a story about a trip she had taken during which she was stuck in traffic for hours because of an accident on one of the bridges leading into the city. Cars were backed up for miles, causing the normal hour drive to take much longer. While narrating her story, she commented on the accident: "It was someone in a rice burner." The inclusion of this detail did not have immediate effect, as evidenced by her continuation of the story. Diana, another white student, turned to Karen with a puzzled expression, her face wrinkled, eyes turned upward, her mouth slightly agape, and asked Karen, "What's a rice burner?" Karen paused in her story, turned to Diana, and casually replied: "Uhm, a Honda. Or some other Japanese car."

Diana's mouth opened farther in what appeared to be astonishment as she stared at Karen, who had since turned back to her original conversational partner, unaware of Diana's look. Diana then replied: "That's *really* bad." At that, Karen again turned around and simply responded that it was a phrase her husband "often uses." Karen's laugh and dismissal of Diana's comment echoed in the room. She looked around and noticed that the class had become silent, all eyes now on her. Diana would later describe in an interview her first reaction to this comment: "It was just like: Do you hear what you just *said*?" Renee, sensing something needed to be done, tried to open up the comment for class discussion, asking the class if "anyone else [had] a problem with this?" The room remained silent. I watched as eyes darted from person to person, then back to Renee. Karen now appeared irritated. Diana continued to glare at Karen, only occasionally looking to Renee.

Karen then stood, saying, "I'm *sorry*," drawing out the words in an exaggerated manner. She then walked to the chalkboard and wrote:

"I will not say rice burner (yada, yada)."

As she stood at the chalkboard, writing next to Renee's "notes" section, the class watched. I looked around at the other students, who had each been previously involved in their own conversations, and noticed the class's attention now focused on the current discussion. Immediately after Karen returned to her seat, visibly irritated, Diana rose from her seat, marched to the chalkboard, and erased "rice burner" and also sat back down. Diana and Karen sat, facing outward, and did not speak again during the class period. The class was completely overtaken by silence until Renee began the day's scheduled lesson.

What does one do with Karen? How should one write Karen in this moment? How does one take the tangle that Karen, in this moment, represents? Karen should be a question for communication and education scholars. She should represent a very complex matrix of normalized discourses, power relations, racist attitudes, and simplistic notions about her own place in the world. The problem with Karen is that she can, in some ways, be simplified, turned into a racist without much room for debate or question. In fact, that she so dramatically and overtly used racist discourse tends to make it easy to dismiss her as a relict of old times, a forgotten era. We can say that "most people would never say that anymore," enjoying the privilege of judging her, placing her in a category of our own desires. We can even, if we are clever, say that that kind of racism is so overt that it is easy to spot, demanding that we instead focus on more subtle forms of racist talk. This kind of dismissal or simplistic analysis only limits the power of Karen's construction. To say her comments in that moment are suggestive of only overt racism is to deny that Karen's talk does not occur in a vacuum; rather, it is part of a larger system of sanctioned talk. Karen's overt comment plays its role within much more subtle forms of the same act. For instance, let's say she commented on the *Indian summer* we are having this season. Or perhaps she noted that she was *gypped* at the store the other day. Perhaps she asks the class: "you *guys* mind if I tell this story?" Note how these comments function exactly the same—they each work to exclude some group in order to privilege another. "Gypped," for instance may not be explicitly violent, but it works in a much more subtle and accepted form. When asked, users may deny its power (as Karen did with her "rice burner" comment), but it works to make possible the kind of exclusion and subsequent privileging that such kinds of language-based performative make possible.

Jessie Daniels, in her book *White Lies*, notes that excluding or dismissing overt acts of racial discourse only ignores the way extreme discourse mirrors mainstream discourse. In this way, it is easy to forget that the act of dismissing them is the way to avoid questioning our own participation in the exact same process. When we dismiss Karen's comments, we only exclude how her comments maintain larger systems of discourse. To analyze Karen properly must not only include a careful critique of her act, but also the ways it is part of a larger process. It is an individual racist performance to be sure, but in our judgment of it as a racist performance, we must not forget that it is part of the process of performativity—the comment is part of the process of racial construction and reiteration. Karen's comment, individual as it is, is part of a larger system of exclusion that works to maintain white privilege. Karen's discourse calls for a complex reading of this moment and how it works to reestablish power.

This kind of analysis is a shift from previous ways of thinking through race and whiteness. It is to turn away from static, fixed locations of whiteness to more constitutive ways of thinking. To label Karen white, to place her discourse choices within a frame of reference (white, privileged, etc.), is to reduce the complexity and remove the acts from their contexts. Karen's comment was so powerful because it was part of a larger system of racial privilege and power. In a way, Karen's own whiteness is the least interesting aspect of this moment—what is more significant is that her discourse feeds into a larger system of power working to maintain power, reifying the very concept of racial hierarchy. It is this process of performativity that this project seeks to study—to work toward a systematic understanding of privilege and power is the goal of this book.

Organization of the Book

I have divided this book into two major sections. In part 1, I sketch out in some detail the turn to performativity as a frame for understanding whiteness. In chapter 1, I discuss what I call the two major treatments of the body in whiteness, calling for a more complex way of seeing whiteness and the body. I move toward what I call the "constitutive body of whiteness," arguing that what the research on whiteness needs is a more performative analysis. To this end, I sketch out Judith Butler's theory of performativity, suggesting that her framework for gender provides a heuristic lens for considering the reproductive nature of whiteness and racial power. I argue that whiteness is a reiterative performance—an identity that is maintained and naturalized through our everyday communication. In chapter 2, I draw out the implications of the reiterative process described in the previous chapter. That is, I claim it is the reproduction of whiteness as purity that is ultimately the outcome of the performative process. To do this, I turn to the specific context of education, examining how education performatively works to erase difference, creating a systematic reproduction of whiteness as a pure educational ideal. The machine of whiteness works, as Butler might suggest, toward an idealized image—an impossible to reach, yet constantly striving toward, goal of whiteness as a pure, clean system.

In part 2 of this project, I turn to my ethnographic research and analyze participants' (re)enactments of whiteness. The classroom I studied was an introductory performance studies classroom entitled "Performing Cultures," in which students learn about culture through performance. Fulfilling a general education requirement at this large Midwestern university, this course asks students to study difference by engaging in performances of poetry, literature, and nonfiction works written by people of diverse cultural backgrounds. The logic in this course is simple and profound: Students learn about culture through others' writings, and if you work toward embodiment of those texts (staged performance), you can gain from a careful analysis of different experiences, lives. My analysis begins in site by looking specifically at students creating these staged, crafted, and prepared performances. Chapter 3 is dedicated to how whiteness gets created and reiterated through these staged messages. Then, chapter 4 continues the analysis by looking at mundane enactments of whiteness, asking how students work to reiterate whiteness through everyday communication. Chapter 5 brings us full circle, returning to my own location in this project. Through autoethnographic poetics, I follow my own ethnographic process during one semester of fieldwork. This chapter asks how the researcher participates in the very process s/he critiques. The book ends with implications, asking how education and cultural critics can address the issues in this book.

*****

I am sitting in a conference, suffering from "hotel-back," preparing to speak this time, doing my thing, my research, my own contribution to the field. The notes before me are typed, black ink on bleached white pages. They begin with a hello, an introduction, and a transition into the first major portion of the essay I have written. The outline continues, taking me to the conclusion—to the ultimate point, argument, nugget of wisdom that people can take away, grasp, or put (as my friend Craig might say) in their go-cup. It is the whole reason for the paper—there, at the end, at the bottom of my bleached white sheet. I close my eyes, waiting for my turn.

Then, I smile. It is a smile of knowing. I smile because I know what I am going to do even as I prepare to do something else—I am going to do whiteness even as I prepare to work against whiteness. Audre Lorde's voice echoes: "The master's tools will never dismantle the master's house." And I smile because I am unsure how to talk about whiteness except through whiteness—how to undermine whiteness except through my own whiteness. I am a paradox. I am searching for the cracks, the gaps in the machinery of whiteness even as I carefully and strategically depend on the logic of whiteness—that linear through-line of classic, rational argumentation. I wonder who is sitting there, in that audience, waiting to call me on it. Who will flinch, this time, at me? Who will make me the star of their writing—the subject of their introduction?

I smile, uncomfortably, and open my eyes in preparation to once again enter the world of paradox, a world I know all too well.

Notes

[1] See Warren ("Social Drama") for a longer examination of Karen and her performatives of whiteness.

Part One

Performativity of Whiteness

Chapter One

Whiteness as a Performative Accomplishment

I love a good metaphor. It sort of just sits there on the tip of the tongue, releasing an intense flavor that captures the essence of what you want to say. Sometimes I struggle with coming up with the right metaphor; other times it just kind of sneaks up on you when you least expect it. Often, I struggle long and hard to find the right words and the right images to convey my metaphorical argument. But the right metaphor is not always a struggle, not always a search. Sometimes it just kind of happens and you are left with a different struggle: a struggle to uncover its meaning.

I was at a conference in Detroit. It was the year for Detroit—I had been there twice in the past several months. It was, however, an appropriate place for the arrival of this metaphor. I was in the lobby of the Hotel Pontchartrain, once the most famous hotel in Detroit. When I told my mother that I would be staying in the Pontch, she told me stories of her time in Detroit before it suffered the pains of white flight and urban decay. The Pontch had been the premier hotel in the city, welcoming all the politicians and celebrities who traveled through. Many a president had stayed in the Pontch, she told me. She also noted that she and my father once ate in the Top of the Pontchartrain, the most elegant restaurant in the city.

As I looked through the lobby, I found it hard to believe that this was the same place my mother had narrated to me. It did have the look of a once-famous hotel, but the temperature in every room was hot and balmy, the rooms smoky and grungy, and the Top of the Pontch was now an empty room occasionally used for banquets. It was no longer the premier hotel in Detroit; of this I was sure. I sat on an old couch, the weight of my body quickly defeating the support mechanisms, the faded fabric stretching to hold me. I placed my briefcase next to me and looked through my bag to find a distraction—something to pass the time between sessions. My choices, which I packed for just this possibility, consisted of the latest Text and Performance Quarterly *and John Hartigan Jr.'s new book,* Racial Situations: Class Predicaments of Whiteness in Detroit. *I thought Hartigan's book would be a good choice, given my trip to Detroit. It was a beautiful book, too. It had a fine, smooth cover, of a slightly off-white color, featuring a picture of "Hillbilly Jerry," a central participant from the book. I picked up both Hartigan's book and the TPQ to peruse them, when I noticed that the rich blue ink from the cover of the TPQ had rubbed off on the back of Hartigan's book. Where there was once the consistent off-white color featuring blue and black lettering, there was now a blue stain across the whole left half of the book. I thought about how that stain might have been created—the books' positions next to each other in the car on the way to the airport, in the plane, and from session to session in the hotel. Slowly, the two had mingled, flirted, and danced in my bag. And through the friction of several days of interaction, the residue of performance was forever stamped on the surface of this book on race and whiteness, never to be the same again.*

Now I won't try to pretend that it was from that moment that I first decided to study the convergence of performance and whiteness, but I will assert that it was in that moment, in that smeared image, that I realized the power of performance as a way of theorizing whiteness. The perfect, although slightly off, whiteness of that book was altered, changed, and stained through its continuous and repeated acts in that bag—those texts rubbed until a noticeable and pronounced mark of color imprinted itself on that book cover. This moment meant a great deal to me as I sat on that faded couch. It continues to affect me as I continue in this line of research. For in that moment, I saw how the whiteness of that book cover was just as constructed as the whiteness of my skin. And my desire to protect it from the stain brought by that journal's color was just as strategic as the incessant acts that continue to protect the purity of whiteness.

No single study, no single manuscript, no single performance ever exists in isolation; rather, it is a product and process built by those that preceded it. Like the multiple, historical, social reiterative acts that have generated whiteness as a cultural signifier of difference, this project is rather a snapshot in the process of my own scholarship examining the performance of identity. Thus, in an effort to properly account for the acts that have preceded this study, I offer a reading of the diverse material that has shaped and made possible this ethnographic excursion. I offer here a new way of seeing whiteness. To this end, I begin with the recent explosion of cultural studies scholarship considering whiteness as a cultural identity, specifically documenting the major treatments of the body in whiteness research: the material body of whiteness and the rhetorical body of whiteness. This brief examination will demonstrate two general trends in scholars' writing that position the body in differing ways. Further, I suggest a third and integrative model that I call the constitutive body of whiteness, drawing most directly from Judith Butler.

The Body in Whiteness

While I use the term "whiteness studies" to describe emergent research on whiteness as a meaningful social construct, the term really constitutes a misnomer and might be a bit premature. More correctly, it falls under the rubric of cultural studies, inspired most significantly by scholars of color who have been writing about the influence of white people on the lives of people of color (see Fanon; hooks, *Yearning*; Morrison; West as examples). Only recently have white (with increased attention from nonwhite) scholars truly engaged whiteness and cultural privilege in critical ways, working to undermine the power of whiteness, which, in racial politics, is often considered the invisible center of Western culture (see Nakayama and Krizek 292-94). Much of this work focuses on the assumption of whiteness as normative and therefore invisible. Peggy McIntosh describes the power of white privilege as an "invisible weightless knapsack" of special tools and provisions that white people can cash in on each and every day without any conscious effort (1-2). In his critical essay "White," Richard Dyer describes whiteness as both invisible and ever present, so much the cultural norm that it ceases to be of notice to white subjects: "This property of whiteness to be everything and nothing is the source of its representational power" (45). Thus, whiteness studies takes as its central mission to mark and thus make visible the unmarked cultural center of power, while also undermining that center by levying detailed descriptions, analyses, and critiques that work to deconstruct the power gained through invisibility.

While multiple writers have published reviews of whiteness literature (see Giroux; Johnson; McLaren, "Decentering"; Rodriguez; Warren, "Whiteness"), none has explored how this scholarship frames the physical body as a social signifier in culture. I first explore what I call the material body of whiteness, in which the body stands as a physical representation of racial identity that carries particular social effects. Second, I consider the body as a rhetorical construction used to levy power. While I present these two foci as independent, I recognize that there is much blurring between them. My divisions are to illuminate how different scholars frame the body in their research. From these two models, I extrapolate and propose an alternative model of the body that moves toward racial performativity. I call this perspective the constitutive body of whiteness.

The Material Body of Whiteness

> I reinhabit a location where black folks associated whiteness with the terrible, the terrifying, the terrorizing. ... [White men's] presence terrified me. Whatever their mission, they looked too much like the unofficial white men who came to enact rituals of terror and torture. (hooks, *Killing* 39)

Performativity grants social agents a conceptual lens for meaningful critique, subversive racial politics, and a transformative social project.

Notes

1   In my work on whiteness, I am reminded of Wallace Bacon's poetic navigation between text and performer ("Dangerous"; "Decade Later"; "One Last Time"). In his struggle between the word and the body, I see my struggle between the rhetorical and the material. And like Bacon, I too am trying to navigate between the "dangerous shores" of these two poles. Also like Bacon, I share the "wondrous" anticipation of bringing the two together for a more complex and potentially rich articulation of our shared political projects.

2   See my essay in *Educational Theory* in which I deconstruct McLaren's (and others') work on white abolitionist projects (Warren, "Performing Whiteness").

3   Certainly, this historical moment was about more than race. Gender, politics, sexuality, and class were all part of what made the Thomas/Hill Senate hearings so problematic. But what Staub foregrounds in his essay is just the way race got made meaningful in those moments, and I think it demonstrates a powerful way of seeing racial production in action. Thomas is a unique figure, brought in clearly to fill Justice Marshall's vacated seat on the bench. His blackness was both exceedingly present in his physical appearance (and served as the reason for his nomination), while also being questioned by those who looked at his cultural politics, noting that his court history did not reflect the concerns of black Americans. Thus, his race was a central issue from the beginning. But when he cited his race and was then so constructed by Hatch, Thomas' Blackness was reaffirmed. As a case study for racial production, Thomas makes for a fascinating subject. However, this does not mean that other social and political factors were not also involved.

4   My effort to work through performativity and whiteness was in the context of race traitors, in which I advocated a more complex reading of whiteness, performativity, and the body. See Warren ("Performing Whiteness") for a different application of this work.

5   My thanks to Craig Gingrich-Philbrook for his help in seeing how Butler's scheme relates to race.

By the "material body of whiteness," I am suggesting several important points. First, I am identifying a research trend that considers the material body—the physical flesh of people—as it relates to studies on race. In other words, how are bodies raced, and how are bodies offered as texts for others' reading? Second, this research examines the effects of racial materiality on social interaction, working to uncover what happens when the physicality of our bodies read differently. Third, whiteness literature that examines race through a frame of bodies' materiality invests itself, even if social construction is its ideological underpinning, in a somewhat stable racial identity. In order for bell hooks, in the preceeding epigraph, to discuss terror, she must rely on a somewhat stable notion of blackness and whiteness, even if she also believes that race is socially negotiated and rhetorically constructed. This research vector strives to understand the effects of bodily interaction by calling attention to our materiality as a socially, culturally meaningful representation. For these reasons, I begin with hooks. Her work on whiteness as terrorism powerfully demonstrates how the materiality of the body—those white bodies that terrorized her—operates as a meaningful text describing what people of color encounter in their daily lives.

One line of research that relies, at least in part, on materiality are essays derived from personal experience, in which an author works to understand the impact of whiteness on his/her own life (see Bérubé with Bérubé; Dunbar; McIntosh; Pelias, *Writing*; Wray). This kind of research requires speaking subjects to name and rely on their own whiteness, describing what happens when the white self reflects on their own skin privilege. The most explicit example of this kind of work is McIntosh's account of her own white privilege, based solely on the materiality of her whiteness. She lists forty-six individual racial privileges granted her because of her ability to pass as white, ranging from not being suspected of shoplifting to being able to buy "flesh" colored bandages that more or less match her skin (5-9). Similarly, Ronald J. Pelias' examination of his watching of *Def Comedy Jam* allows for a concrete example of how one's materiality—Pelias' body and the bodies of the comics on television—stands as a site of social critique on race. In this poetic essay, Pelias juxtaposes the writing of bell hooks against his voyeuristic viewing of the black comedians on television to determine how his whiteness stands in relation to the blackness he sees there. The separation of his whiteness, the black comedians, and the appeal to bell hooks as an authoritative black scholarly voice relies on the materiality of flesh, locating the signifier of difference between black and white most pronounced in the appearance of bodies.

While personal experience serves as the location of critique for both Pelias and McIntosh, many scholars locate their own materiality in relation to their speaking/writing voices. Such positioning serves to locate their researching bodies, calling attention to (and thus a reliance on) the materiality of their own racial identities. For instance, Ruth Frankenberg begins her book by locating her voice "as a white feminist" (3). Richard Dyer also begins with a statement about his own awareness of whiteness, arguing that as a white gay man he feels a certain amount of kinship with nonwhites. In her study of white supremacy, Jessie Daniels notes her difficulty in coming to terms with a linkage in her family history to white supremacy movements. Christine E. Sleeter notes that she writes as "a Euroamerican person who has struggled with [her] own understanding of race" ("How White" 168). Alice McIntyre dedicates a whole chapter in her book to developing her speaking positionality, noting that she enters the field as an "educator, a white North American, working-class feminist, who has been afforded multiple opportunities in this society" (29). Each of these works, regardless of topic, makes explicit the author's own identity by calling attention to his or her material whiteness.

Several education scholars have spent considerable time uncovering how whiteness plays itself out in educational systems. From Linda C. Powell's essay on whiteness and black underachievement to Frances Maher and Mary Kay Thompson Tetreault's ethnographic work in classrooms to Elizabeth Ellsworth's work on the performative double binds of whiteness, scholars seek to understand how race functions as a system of advantage and disadvantage based on the materiality of the raced body. In particular, Sleeter has written extensively on whiteness and the predicament of white teachers ("How White" and *Multicultural*), suggesting that "educators of color are much more likely to bring life experiences and viewpoints that critique white supremacy than are white teachers" ("How White" 169). While Sleeter's desire to diversify the teaching force is admirable and indeed needed, her solution to racism in education demonstrates a powerful reliance on the physical features of the material body.

Studies that take the materiality of the body as a primary concern appear to claim or describe their subjects as stable raced bodies. For instance, in a study of white identity development at historically black universities, Ronald L. Jackson II conducted focus groups with "white students," looking to see if they undergo code-switching like black students do in mainstream universities (45). His findings support the general body of whiteness literature, in which white individuals support ideals of individualism and cultural dominance. Yet the way Jackson seamlessly defines whiteness and blackness in an effort to ask particular political and academic questions demonstrates the easy way of understanding racial identity, primarily on the basis of materiality. Mark P. Orbe relies on the material appearance of race as the qualifier for categorization in his study of African American male communication patterns, counting on the stability of blackness (and the participants' stable understandings of whiteness) for his findings. Jackson's and Orbe's work, while not entirely in the tradition of whiteness studies, demonstrates that a reliance on the material body of whiteness as a starting point of one's research falls into essentialist traps that render race primarily in the physical.

Several studies work on whiteness from psychological development models, examining "white identity ego levels" (see Carter; Helms; Tatum). These models allow people to see the development of white identity as it progresses through stages of race awareness, beginning with "contact" and working toward "autonomy" (Carter 201-5). While the developmental process provides space for individuals to become aware of and respond to psychological concerns of race, the models depend on an already established white subject. Robert C. Carter describes level two, "disintegration," as the moment when the "individual learns that race does matter, that racism does exist, and [he or she is] white" (202). Carter's whole schema relies on easy notions of race that locate racial identity primarily in the body. In Beverly Daniel Tatum's essay on teaching white students about racism, she outlines three models for whiteness: the racist white supremacist, the "what whiteness?" model, and the guilty white. She goes on to suggest a need for the white ally, calling for a "pro-active white identity" (472). Each of her models, while serving as helpful ways of conceptualizing how people enact (or could enact) their whiteness, relies so heavily on a stable racial identity that whiteness appears completely fixed in the materiality of the body.

Certainly, the scholarship I have described covers diverse issues, yet is interrelated by locating race in the materiality of bodies as physical representations of color. Thus, the research described here all depends, in some way, on the body as a visible and stable representation of race categories. These authors would not necessarily claim that the body carries some biological necessity that dictates race, but rather that we, as a society with a history of racial inequality, have constructed visual categories or prototypes that provide a lens for reading people's race. Consequently, even though these authors might argue that racial meaning can be socially constructed, they still rely on the physicality of our bodies, usually foregrounding skin pigment in the service of political action. The desire to focus on the material body of whiteness often has to do with the political, everyday consequences of race in this social world.

The Rhetorical Body of Whiteness

> Whiteness, thus, is not merely a discourse that is contained in societies inhabited by white people; it is not a phenomenon that is enacted only where white bodies exist. Whiteness is not just about bodies and skin color, but rather more about the *discursive practices* that, because of colonialism and neocolonialism, privilege and sustain the global dominance of white imperial subjects and Eurocentric worldviews. (Shome, "Whiteness" 108, emphasis in original)

I begin this section on the "rhetorical body" with a quotation from communication theorist Raka Shome (see also Shome, "Race"), because she frames how this trend in scholarship positions the body as a rhetorical construct. I use "rhetoric" here in two key ways. First, I frame this research in terms of discourse, or the communicative systems of whiteness that influence our understandings of race. Second, I suggest rhetoric as a way of knowing, in which whiteness is an epistemological construction. In other words, what are the ways whiteness comes to have meaning in the Western social world? The rhetorical body in this sense is a discursive construction that works to levy power and influence through communicative means. This levying of power can occur through either ascription or avowal—that is, one can either ascribe identity to another through some sort of naming or avow an identity through self-identification (Martin et al). In both cases, the power to name serves as a discursive construction of whiteness. Thus, by "body," I am not suggesting physical flesh but rather the discursively constructed body, an ideal or archetypal conception that is used to levy discursive power. The following studies all frame whiteness as a discursive power, a location that does not rely on some inherent identity embedded in the body, but one that functions in communicative interaction in which individuals cite or appeal to this discourse as a way to wield power. As Shome notes above, whiteness is a discourse that works to retain power and privilege within those subjects that can and do claim the power of whiteness. This research uses the metaphor of space or cultural position, which removes the focus of whiteness from the "white" appearing subject while focusing attention on the power that is levied from that subject position (Naka-yama and Krizek 291). Shome importantly notes in the opening epigraph that the body is not absent in this research, but rather, that whiteness consists of more than the representational color of one's skin. Whiteness is the discursive force behind that subjectivity. Shome goes on to say that—

> whiteness needs to be studied through the *interlocking axes of power, spatial location, and his-tory*. This recognition—the relation among white domination, history, and spatial loca-tion—encourages a nonessentialist and a historically specific understanding of white-ness. ("Whiteness" 109, emphasis in original)

The clearest example of this work is Nakayama and Krizek's essay "White-ness: A Strategic Rhetoric." Working with the spatial metaphor allows them to "rethink the ways in which individuals and groups construct identity, administer power, and make sense of their everyday lives" that do not place identity in the materiality of their bodies (291). In other words, the focus of their empirical work is not based in the fact of their participants' whiteness, but in how they use or cite a discourse that works to promote and maintain white privilege and power. Nakayama and Krizek provided open-ended surveys to white students, asking them to describe how they racially identify themselves. Note here the messiness of categorizing this work. By relying on the stability of "white" stu-dents for their surveys, Nakayama and Krizek do rely on the stability and mate-riality of racial identity. However, I locate this essay in the rhetorical body sec-tion of the review because their essay considers how these participants describe and talk about their identities, using differing strategies and labels to accomplish different rhetorical purposes. Thus, the study attempts to determine how this collection of folks levy power through their "strategies that mark the space of whiteness" (292). Given this focus, I locate their essay as an analysis of the rhe-torical body of whiteness, remembering that while these categories illuminate differences, they also obscure similarities.

Nakayama and Krizek then analyzed the responses, providing six distinct and specific ways these students talked about race that worked to promote and protect whiteness's power. One of the six strategies of the discourse of white-ness was a connection of whiteness to power. In other words, students used words like "majority" or "dominant" to describe whiteness. What this strategy, as well as the other five, accomplishes is a protection of whiteness's discursive strength. By locating whiteness in a rhetorical discursive space, the study advances an understanding of whiteness as a rhetorical body of power.

In the field of literary criticism, Toni Morrison's book *Playing in the Dark* examines American fiction to see how it rhetorically influences our understanding of racial hierarchies. In this book, Morrison discusses the metaphors of whiteness and blackness in literature, claiming that all American literature positions the reader as white (xii). By both naming and locating the characters in literature as white and by assumptions made about the reader, this study, like most other work in the rhetorical body of whiteness, uncovers how a particular kind of discourse promotes and maintains white dominance. By assuming whiteness, the literary imagination secures and protects whiteness's power as the dominant racial category.

Morrison's work, in many ways, argues that whiteness gains its power through universalizing the rhetorical body of whiteness—that the readers and characters inhabit a universally white space where whiteness is discursively constructed as the norm. This argument echoes Warren Montag's argument about whiteness:

> To be white is to be human, and to be human is to be white. In this way, the concept of whiteness is deprived of its purely racial character at the moment of its universalization, no longer conceivable as a particularistic survival haunting the discourse of universality but, rather, as the very form of human universality itself. (285)

What is so remarkable in this brief section from Montag's essay is the discursive power he locates in whiteness. His removal of whiteness from the material body as a racialized subject to a rhetorical body of discourse in which humanity is universally positioned as white creates a vision of whiteness as a power-laden force that grants privilege and dominance to white subjects.

For many scholars, connecting white subjectivity to white bodies is a problem. For instance, AnnLouise Keating, responding almost directly to hooks' notion of whiteness as cultural terrorism, fears that such a conflation of whiteness and individual white folks "implies that all human beings classified as 'white' *automatically* exhibit the traits associated with 'whiteness': They are, by *nature*, insidious, superior, empty, terrible, terrifying, and so on" (907, emphasis in original). Keating's desire to separate the discourse of whiteness from white people represents her desire to focus on the rhetorical body—that spatial system of power and influence levied or cited by individuals—while leaving the material body aside. Her concern that the discourse of whiteness might affect our understandings of the materiality of whiteness asserts itself as the strongest separation of these two heuristic categories.

Finally, Ruth Frankenberg's powerfully written and often-cited book, *White Women, Race Matters*, strongly exhibits what I call the rhetorical body of whiteness by framing whiteness as a social construction that goes far beyond the materiality of the body:

> Whiteness . . . has a set of linked dimensions. First, whiteness is a location of structural advantage, of race privilege. Second, it is a "standpoint," a place from which white people look at [themselves], at others, and at society. Third, "whiteness" refers to a set of cultural practices that are usually unmarked and unnamed. (1)

From the start, Frankenberg locates whiteness as a rhetorical construction consisting of "cultural practices" providing "structural advantage" on which "white people" stand. This positioning, while in some ways relying on a stable notion of whiteness, does focus on the power exerted by this social position. Her method involves interviewing "thirty white women" on their understandings of race and their own cultural identity (23). While her book explores several dimensions of these women's lives, a key section consists of her analysis of how these women think through race—how they make sense of their own whiteness. Her results range from "color evasion," a dodging of difference where by one claims color blindness, resulting in an escape from the whole issue of racism, to "race cognizance," a rich understanding of the power of whiteness and how they, as individuals, benefit from racism coupled with a commitment to undermine systems of domination (142-57). What I find significant is the connection between Frankenberg's work and McIntyre's "white talk," a form of communication used by whites to deny their own culpability for racism. Both scholars focus on social interaction, situating their analysis of whiteness in power levied through talk and gesture by white subjects.

The works described above, while covering varying topics through various methods, all appeal to the rhetorical body, that system of discourse that levies power and influence through human agents. Thus, the rhetorical body of whiteness functions as a discourse, a fluid sea of values, beliefs, and practices that individuals draw upon, consciously or unconsciously, to exert cultural power and maintain a racial system that keeps whiteness safe as the cultural center. The scholars who view whiteness as rhetorical consider the focus on the material body too easy, arguing that the rhetoric of whiteness does not necessarily need a materially white body for that person to promote the values, beliefs, and practices embedded in whiteness. For instance, the rhetoric of politician Alan Keyes, a black conservative who often bids for the Republican presidential nomination, cites or appeals to the same principles of individualism and meritocracy that whites do. The "fact" of his blackness does not mean that he does not promote and sustain the same power relations as a rhetoric of whiteness. The rhetorical body of whiteness is a discourse that can be and is cited by anyone with similar effects, regardless of skin pigment.

Toward a Constitutive Body of Whiteness

> The presence of black people in ... films allows one to see whiteness as whiteness, and in this way relates to the existential psychology that is at the origins of the interest in "otherness" as an explanatory concept in the representation of ethnicity. (Dyer, "White" 48).

As research initiatives, both the material body of whiteness and the rhetorical body of whiteness draw critics. Keating argues that skin color and the individual's actions and thoughts are not causally connected: "The fact that a person is born with 'white' skin does not necessarily mean that s/he will think, act, and write in the 'white' ways" (907). She goes on to suggest that white skin does not necessarily cause individuals to levy whiteness in such oppressive ways. On the other hand, Dreama Moon articulates the problem of denying the materiality of race: "While I agree that it is important not to conflate [whiteness and white people], I would argue that it is politically unwise to pretend that white *people* somehow are not implicated in the everyday production and reproduction of 'whiteness'" (179, emphasis in original).

Suggesting a third, more dialectical, perspective of race and the body, some scholars find that by using the material body in order to demonstrate rhetorical social effects, one can create a powerful and complex consideration of whiteness. I call this third understanding of whiteness the "constitutive body of whiteness" because it attempts a more complex reading of whiteness that focuses on how meaning gets made on/through physical bodies. As of yet, this perspective is most clear in film theory, where scholars look at the representation of material whiteness in an effort to see how this discursively constructs our understandings of race. Film provides a distinct example of material representations of race that can then be examined as rhetorical manifestations of power (see Madison). Consider the epigraph from Dyer that frames this section.

In his consideration of film and the representations of bodies through that medium, he finds that cinema powerfully teaches people about race, by rhetorically constructing whiteness through the representation of white bodies. In his book *White*, Dyer unravels the ways raced bodies get wrapped in a discourse of power that helps shape peoples' understandings of race. For example, in a chapterlong discussion of the fourteen-episode English television series *The Jewel in the Crown*, Dyer explores how the repetition of the line "There's nothing I can do!" helps contribute to rhetorical constructions of whiteness's relationship to racism through the central white female character, who is without agency through the duration of the serial. His work also examines whiteness and Christianity by exploring how the Virgin Mary is represented in art as the ultimate pure, white figure, arguing that these images help to constitute the "white ideal" (*White* 17). While the book covers a variety of topics, Dyer continually returns to the material representations of white bodies in order to demonstrate how a rhetorical body of whiteness gets constituted through these texts. Critics like hooks and Dyer advocate critical/cultural analysis of film, television, and other popular texts to uncover how representations of class, race, gender, and sexuality work to promote or resist oppressive systems of dominance (see hooks, *Outlaw*).

Communication research on whiteness in film explores how these popular texts represent race (see Crenshaw; S. Jackson, "White"; Madison; Projansky and Ono). While Dyer considers representations of whiteness in film, these studies explicitly examine how these texts construct rhetorical messages, focusing on our interaction with film as a communicative process. For instance, Shome discusses whiteness as represented in *City of Joy*, arguing that the 1992 film participates in a construction of the white savior who travels to distant lands to find his salvation:

> The problem with such representations of white identity as a savior to humanity is not only that it perpetuates a timeless myth about the apparent superiority of whiteness but that it also legitimizes a rhetoric of liberal white paternalism. ("Race" 504)

Shome powerfully notes how *City of Joy* fits within a genre of films that feature the white savior entering the wilderness filled with savages of color to find his or her own salvation by saving others. It is through the consideration of how whiteness gets constituted that makes this analysis so important.

Henry A. Giroux adds to the scholarship examining whiteness in film by exploring how the body of LouAnne Johnson in the film *Dangerous Minds* (1995) gets constituted. This piece nicely alludes to the constitutive body of whiteness by locating LouAnne's white body in a classroom filled with students of color. The juxtaposition of the authoritative white body of the teacher, played by Michelle Pfeiffer, and the Latino and black students is a sharp contrast both physically and through their manner of social interaction. While LouAnne speaks standard English, desires academic success, and embodies the Western notion of the civilized, rational individual, the students are violent, poorly educated (in the academic sense), vulgar, and powerfully representative of criminality and danger (303). Giroux's analysis skillfully positions the materiality of the bodies in the film as rhetorical choices about what urban education is like, connecting whiteness with civility and blackness and Latino culture with savagery.

A more constitutive approach to whiteness allows one to see how both the rhetorical and material dimensions of raced bodies can combine to generate powerful readings of the body. Such a conceptualization of the body in whiteness steers away from the pitfalls of essentialism that the material body risks, while also denying that white people, and the privilege that subject position is granted, are completely unconnected to the racism perpetuated by the ideology of whiteness.[1] Further, the constitutive body of whiteness also demonstrates how an analysis might go beyond the binary of material and rhetorical to see how the material itself comes to flesh through discursive communicative messages. The constitutive body of whiteness asks about how whiteness comes to be, and with that focus lies its subversive potential. It is in the spirit of these early writings that I turn to performativity, a theoretical lens that allows for a more dialectical understanding of racial constitution. Performativity moves a conversation about the body in whiteness (in both its corporeality and its rhetorical abstractedness) toward understanding how such subjectivities are constructed in the first place. As one considers the potential of a more constitutive body of whiteness, the language and theoretical sophistication of performativity most accurately describe how such meanings are brought to bear on the physical body.

Performative Repetitions of Racial Identity

It is only through [the] disavowal that . . . whiteness is constituted, and through the institutionalization of that disavowal that . . . whiteness is perpetually—but anxiously—reconstituted. (Butler, *Bodies* 171)

I begin with a statement from Judith Butler, for I locate the vision of my scholarship in her writing. Indeed, it is her work with performativity, and the promise I see in that work for critical race studies, that draws me to performativity. Butler establishes a way of seeing not only how race comes to matter but how race is (re)constituted through the act of disavowal. I will return to this quotation later in this section.

While my work explicitly advocates a turn toward racial performativity, several scholars have already either claimed performativity, alluded to cultural performance, or at least suggested a possible performative reading in their work. For instance, Peter McLaren argues that whiteness is perpetuated through a continued embodiment of whiteness, suggesting that one may choose "against whiteness" ("Decentering" 10; "Unthinking" 38). While McLaren provides little or no guidance on what choosing "blackness or brownness" really means for folks who still read culturally as white (10), he does begin to suggest a more performative approach to race as a cultural accomplishment.[2] John Hartigan Jr., a cultural ethnographer who studies whiteness in social and cultural contexts, conducted an extensive study of race in Detroit ("Locating"; "Name Calling"; *Racial*). While his analysis is more constitutive in that he situates his study in the participants' rhetorical constructions of whiteness through the materiality of their own white bodies, his work does begin to suggest my interest in performativity through his discussion of how class alters the performance of white identity. In "Locating White Detroit," this focus becomes the most clear when Hartigan juxtaposes "suburban whites" and "poor whites," pointing to how differences in socioeconomic conditions affect how one accomplishes or constructs one's whiteness (187). While these works suggest a performative reading, McLaren and Hartigan do not explicitly locate their work as performative.

Ironically, I find the most interesting source for a performative reading of whiteness to be essays not constructed by, or even using the language of, performativity. In his essay on the white gaze and Rush Limbaugh, David R. Roediger constructs a powerful argument detailing the performative constitution of whiteness through embodiment. Roediger begins by setting the stage of Limbaugh's television show, where Limbaugh powerfully constructs whiteness through his "white look" (42). Limbaugh's show, Roediger argues, carries segments in which clips of liberal politicians ("the left") are played through a split-screen in which Limbaugh proceeds to jeer at and mock the speaker, who is recorded on video and therefore unable to respond to Limbaugh's attacks. In one particular instance, Limbaugh mocks one of his favorite targets, Dr. Joycelyn Elders, a professional black woman who speaks in medical terminology as the Surgeon General. In these segments, she shares a split screen with Limbaugh, who is mocking her every move. This kind of gesturing to Elders' image, which is similar to his nonverbal mocking of Jesse Jackson's vocal qualities, works to construct Limbaugh's whiteness in powerful ways. By disassociating himself from those figures of color in those highly performative moments, he constructs their blackness through his jeering gaze as that which not only deserves insult but is also so foreign or "other" that his intense, direct disciplinary gaze is required to performatively code that blackness as ridiculous. The mocking response from Limbaugh, followed by a rational critique of his own position, frames blackness, and those highly positioned African Americans, as inferior to Limbaugh's own rational whiteness—he gets to critique the speakers of "the left" while providing his audience with a conservative position that is never held to the same standard as that which he levies at others. In this way, Limbaugh maintains his critical gaze without worrying about any possible reciprocation.

Michael E. Staub's work on the Anita Hill and Clarence Thomas controversy during Thomas' confirmation hearings to the Supreme Court in 1991 provides another performative look at whiteness. During Thomas' testimony, Orrin Hatch, a powerful white Republican senator, responded to Thomas' claim that Hill was playing into a racial stereotype by saying:

> What an interesting concept that you have just raised. ... When you talk in terms of stereotypes, what are you saying here? I mean I want to understand this. ... You said some of this language is stereotype language? What does this mean, I don't understand. (53)

What I find so incredibly powerful in both Hatch's statement and Staub's analysis is the degree to which Thomas and Hatch performatively made race present in these remarks. That comment by Hatch, built from the foundation established by Thomas, discursively made Thomas the expert on blackness; Hill a traitor to her race (through her criticisms of Thomas), who does her own blackness incorrectly (which Thomas was forced to correct); and Hatch the patient, concerned antiracist in need of being educated by Thomas' authoritative experience as a black man.[3] Staub argues that Hatch's comment served to "set up Thomas as the expert on anything relating to blackness, establishing his rendition of his own life as unchallengeable by any white man" (53). Thus, Hatch performatively made his own whiteness distinct from, and opposite to, Thomas' blackness through his "confusion" over the daily strife of blackness.

Building from these works, I now turn to Judith Butler's writing to flesh out and give form to my understanding of whiteness as a performative process. In *Bodies That Matter*, Butler dedicates a chapter to Nella Larsen's novella *Passing* in which Larsen powerfully uncovers how whiteness gets constituted in the act of passing. Butler acknowledges two key characteristics about Claire, a woman who passes as white throughout the novella. First, Claire is a "black woman" who regularly passes as white; and second, Bellew, Claire's white husband, calls her "Nig," even before he learns of her blackness, suggesting at least some kind of recognition of Claire's lightly colored body. Claire and Irene, another African American, continue to pass as white throughout the story, although Irene warns that Claire passes too much (*Bodies* 170). As Butler's analysis proceeds, she discusses how race gets constituted through Claire's and Irene's passing. Butler argues:

> Claire passes not only because she is light-skinned, but because she refuses to introduce her blackness into conversation and so withholds the conversational marker which would counter the hegemonic presumption that she is white. Irene herself appears to "pass" insofar as she enters conversations which presume whiteness as the norm without contesting that assumption. This dissociation from blackness that she performs through silence is reversed at the end of the story in which she is exposed to Bellew's white gaze in clear associations with African Americans. It is only on the condition of an association that conditions a naming that her color becomes legible. He cannot "see" her as black before that association. (171)

In this analysis, Butler uncovers how whiteness functions as a discursive performative accomplishment. Not only did Claire and Irene actively participate in their passing by refusing to assert their blackness, but Bellew's recognition of Claire's blackness through the nickname "Nig" demonstrates how, through the act of engaging in conversation with and marrying a woman of color, he participates in the making of both Claire's and Irene's whiteness. This example, by denying the essentialized notion that race exists prior to our expression of it, provides a glimpse at the power of a performative analysis of whiteness. I will return periodically to this passage in order to tease out some of the characteristics of performativity.

Performativity,[4] a concept with ties to J. L. Austin's speech act theory, basically takes the material argument, detailed in part by the scholars discussed above, and turns it on its head. Austin examined language by creating a typology of the functions of words and their effects. He found that certain words accomplish action through the articulation of the linguistic construction itself. His most famous example is the wedding ceremony, in which the marriage is accomplished through the saying of "I now pronounce you husband and wife." He argued that the act was indeed accomplished through the saying, moving the discipline of linguistics to consider how words function as acts in and of themselves. Much of Judith Butler's work extends and complicates Austin's initial work with language, connecting the performative nature of language to the process of identity constitution. On the most elemental level, Butler examines the function of naming, arguing that naming serves an interpellative function: "Naming is at once a setting of a boundary, and also a repeated inculcation of a norm" (*Bodies* 8). From Austin's early work examining particular performatives (e.g., the wedding pronouncement), Butler makes the extension to account for the more mundane performative nature of our language. This work is continued by Butler in *Excitable Speech*, where she notes again the performative nature of naming: "Being called a name is also one of the conditions by which a subject is constituted in language" (2). In each of these examples, naming—the linguistic offering of a possible identity—aids in the constitution of identity. From Austin's early work, theories of the performative have grown to account for the mundane maintenance of identity.

Butler ultimately defines performativity "not [as] a singular act, for it is always a reiteration of a norm or set of norms" (*Bodies* 12). Connecting to our theorizing of race, performativity demands a reversal of traditional theories of race: Rather than arguing that we read race from bodies, which assumes that race somehow exists prior to our reading, theories of performativity argue that race comes to exist through our expression of it. Race is constituted through the repetition of acts, verbal and nonverbal, that continue to communicate difference. In Butler's often-cited essay "Performative Acts and Gender Constitution," she describes gender performatively, as "a *stylized repetition of acts*" (270, emphasis in original). Through Butler's work, one can see a complex understanding of what enactment entails. If we look at race as a stylized repetition of acts, in which the gestures, movements, and other kinds of communication constitute meaning, then race as an identifier of difference is not *in* the body but rather made *through* bodily acts. This is to say, the repeated performance of race creates an illusion of substance that appears bodily ("Performative" 271). Thus, the body is raced inasmuch as we successfully accomplish the appearance of race through our enactments.

The raced body as a performative accomplishment depends on the repetitiousness of acts, for it is in the repeated nature that identities become normalized. Here, like layers of sand constituting a rock, the repeated enactments of identity become sedimented and seemingly fixed, as if they had always been there. Taken as rock, the process of sedimentation—of normalization over time—loses its historical nature. This normalization of the repeated acts of race serves to hide or obfuscate its construction. Like gender, race "is thus a construction that regularly conceals its genesis," obscuring the process in favor of surface appearances ("Performative" 273). Again, I turn to Butler to describe the effect of this repetitive citational practice:

> The name has, thus, a historicity, what might be understood as the history which has become internal to a name, has come to constitute the contemporary meaning of a name: the sedimentation of its usages as they have become part of the very name, a sedimentation, a repetition that congeals, that gives the name its force. (*Excitable* 36)

As Butler notes, it is the repeated nature of these acts that grants them so much power. Each time the citation of identity is offered, it carries with it the power of history, building the force of those repeated acts until the discursive construction begins to look so natural that its construction is completely petrified, solidified.

To demonstrate the stability upon which such constructions lie, Butler shows that one of the key ways identity becomes normalized through such repetition is through social consequences. To fail to do one's race correctly calls upon a system of punishments that reinforce and reinscribe the very illusion of race as something that exists outside of our continual acts that maintain it. If one fails to do his/her whiteness correctly, s/he is held accountable for that transgression, which can range from subtle looks, harsh words, or physical attacks. This kind of punishment system only serves to stabilize race, allowing it to appear natural.

Take for instance, the performativity of race through Ebonics. One of the ways people know that this kind of speech is associated with blackness is the repeated acts that continue to mark it as a characteristic of people of African descent. In other words, the repeated acts of hearing African Americans use it, watching the news and hearing the debates about it and its effects on black children, and seeing representations of it on television sitcoms and the like continually mark that discourse as black. In that repetitive act, the connection of Ebonics to blackness becomes so normalized, so mundane, that it generates the appearance of being the "natural" way African Americans talk. But a performative analysis would argue that it is the repeated acts—the continual act of Ebonics by black-identified people and the connection of Ebonics and black folk by popular culture—that constructs blackness as a possible racial identity. Indeed, the raised eyebrows from the white community about using Ebonics as a teaching tool was a question of identity, for in schools, where whiteness is normalized, the use of black vernacular would question the legitimacy of standard American English and the very whiteness of the schooling system itself. It is the naming—the continual and repeated efforts to locate identity prior to (and as the cause of) the speech pattern—that reduces this complex set of racial performatives to essentialism. Butler's reformation of identity shifts away from essentialism and toward the power of discursive sedimentation as an explanation for how these namings, these citations of identity, come to have meaning.

Butler concentrates much of her analysis on the materiality of the body. She does this, in part, to explain how performativity accounts for the physicality of the body as a historical project. A performative analysis of the white body situates the body in time, acknowledging that the materiality of the body can be seen as a repetition of discursive acts. For instance, an examination of my body next to an African American's body—my white skin juxtaposed to his/her black skin—would reveal different pigments to be sure. But, by placing our bodies in historical context, it requires that one see how our bodies were created in the first place. In other words, my family history consists of millions of acts where by decisions were made about who may mate with whom. The fact of my whiteness is not accidental; "nature has a history," cautioned Butler (*Bodies* 5). Rather, my whiteness is an accomplishment of a history of normalized discursive moments that worked together to make me appear this skin tone. The fact of my materiality is a "continual and incessant *materializing* of possibilities" ("Performative" 272, emphasis in original). The outcome that is the material body is, in the end, a fulfillment of a historical possibility. This is one key way that scholars of race/whiteness could meaningfully discuss bodies in which both the materiality and the impact of historical and social power are brought to light.

To help flesh out a conceptual framework for understanding the racial body, I offer an adaptation of Butler's performative reformulation of bodies.[5] In *Bodies That Matter*, Butler concentrates on the materiality of the body but argues that "materiality will be rethought as the effect of power, as power's most productive effect" (2). Thus the body's physicality is repositioned not as a starting point, but rather as the effect of a discourse of power that has regulated, shaped, and made the materiality of our bodies. She offers five key stakes in such a consideration of bodies, which I will read through the lens of race and whiteness. First at stake in reformulating bodies, is "the recasting of the matter of bodies as the effect of a dynamic of power, such that the matter of bodies will be indissociable from the regulatory norms that govern their materialization and signification of those material effects" (2). Butler repositions bodies as the effect of regulatory norms that have historically dictated (and continue, for the most part, to dictate) the practices that constitute race. This is to say, the color of one's skin cannot be separated from the practices that have historically constructed it—pigment is a product of a stylized repetition of acts.

Second, Butler contends that "the understanding of performativity not as the act by which a subject brings into being what s/he names, but, rather, as that reiterative power of discourse to produce the phenomena that it regulates and controls" is at stake in reformulating the materiality of bodies (2). When Peter McLaren advocates rejecting whiteness in his article "Decentering Whiteness," he paints a very limited picture of how race is accomplished. I can't magically rename my race; I cannot decide to be other than white just by saying it. Rather, I am part of a social system that continually, through both strategic means and mundane enactments, reiterates my whiteness. My own performance of identity is, in part, constituted through the performative acts of others. Take for instance the "wigger" phenomenon that is taking place in many upper/middle-class suburban communities, in which white teens are actively listening to hip-hop music and wearing the latest hip-hop clothing. This is an example of cultural appropriation, an ownership of an identity without the political necessity for it, as well as an example of a performative construction of self that heavily relies on the performance of others (Hartigan, *Racial* 322). Thus, I was born into a performative discursive system that affects my actions, desires, and speech (as well as others' actions, desires, and speech) in such a way as to continue to produce the effects of whiteness.

The third stake in reformulating bodies is "the construal of ['race'] no longer as a bodily given on which the construct of [whiteness] is artificially imposed, but as a cultural norm which governs the materialization of bodies" (2-3). Here, the fact of my whiteness can no longer be traced back to an assumption of an already raced body. Rather, whiteness becomes the cultural norm—I do whiteness through my choice of whom to marry, my choice of whom to reproduce with, and my everyday choices that help to reproduce an illusion of racial stability. These performative possibilities, furthermore, are made possible precisely because the norms are so powerfully imposed. So if I choose to reproduce with someone who is nonwhite, my choice is still a reproduction of a cultural possibility constituted by whiteness. To act against a norm is to reproduce the norm, regardless of intent. It is the cultural illusion of racial purity that governs the color of bodies.

Fourth, another stake in reformulating bodies is "a rethinking of the process by which a bodily norm is assumed, appropriated, taken on as not, strictly speaking, undergone by a subject, but rather that the subject, the speaking 'I,' is formed by virtue of having gone through such a process, of assuming a [race]" (3). In Butler's rather dense passage, she reconceptualizes the formation of subjectivity. She argues against the notion that a white subject undergoes the bodily norm of whiteness, because that assumes an already formed subject. Conceived performatively, subjectivity is itself formed by going through such a process. Butler argues that my white subjectivity is not something "I" underwent, but rather, by undergoing the process of white subjectivity, my "I" was formed—an "I" that is, in and of itself, a product of the social, political, and cultural possibilities generated through history. In other words, people constitute their racial subjectivity through the maintenance and regulation of racial norms.

Finally, Butler offers, in my estimation, the key to performativity by locating the reconceptualization of bodies as "a linking of this process of 'assuming' a [race] with the question of *identification*, and with the discursive means by which the [white] imperative enables certain [raced] identifications and forecloses and/or disavows other identifications" (3, emphasis in original). I find this statement powerful because it establishes race as a relation between (at least) two seemingly separate entities. Thinking about race as a relation provides a lens that allows one to examine how race gets made through specific acts of (re)naming difference. Simply put, race exists only inasmuch as it exists in difference to something else. Whiteness doesn't exist in a vacuum but in relation to nonwhiteness. By uncovering the ways that "white" persons either identify or disavow others, one works to uncover some of the mundane ways people produce race. For instance, in Larsen's *Passing*, whiteness gets constituted through the identification made by Bellew. The acts of conversation and eventual marriage with Claire, given Bellew's strict policy of refusing interaction with people of color, performatively construct Claire's whiteness. Her whiteness, constituted through a specific and highly fashioned repetition of acts, is challenged only when someone names Claire's blackness. When Bellew shifts from an identification with her whiteness to a recognition or marking of difference, Claire ceases to be white.

Building from this last point in Butler's reformulation of bodies, Elin Diamond's separation of performance and performativity gains importance. The turn to identification and disavowal as discrete acts (which together constitute a normalizational process) suggests the power of examining the process through the individual act. Thus, Diamond defines performativity as the process of repetition by which norms are constituted; however, a performance is one reiteration (one single enactment) within that process. Diamond then concludes that the singular performance "is precisely the site in which concealed or dissimulated conventions might be investigated" (5). This is significant—it is here that my analysis takes flight. In this project, I turn to the acts themselves, asking how a careful reading and analysis of the acts—the individually performed acts of whiteness—help to re-create the system of racism. For if we return to Butler's quotation that began this section, we can see how this project seeks to interrupt the process through the localized act. Butler argues: "It is only through [the] disavowal that . . . whiteness is constituted, and through the institutionalization of that disavowal that . . . whiteness is perpetually—but anxiously—reconstituted" (Butler, *Bodies* 171). In locating and critically analyzing how whiteness gets made—what acts help to construct race—we have hope. That is, we have hope for different ways of seeing, speaking, and being. Performativity, unlike the other models or trends I identified earlier, makes space for coming to constitute whiteness (and race) differently. Unlike the material body of whiteness, performativity does not invest the body with such an essentialized representation of race that its meaningfulness cannot be unmade. Unlike the rhetorical body of whiteness, performativity does not grant such power to the system that one feels caught in a power structure that is almost impossible to change. Rather, performativity understands race to be the naturalized appearance of substance; it understands race as a constructed historical and social project, not a fixed system of power. We see the effects of a legacy of performative acts, which means that because race and whiteness are made, they are "capable of being constituted differently" ("Performative" 271). Ultimately, if we uncover how race gets made and how the social, cultural meaningfulness of whiteness maintains its power, then, as agents in the world, we can struggle to change.

Chapter Two

The Performativity of Purity

The other day, I was teaching. My class consists of about thirty undergraduate students, most of whom are education majors. This class, "Education and Society," is a junior-level course— a two-hour class on Tuesday nights—and is the only course dedicated to issues of culture and society in the education curriculum at my university. Today, I am showing a video, a documentary from Los Angeles after the passage of Proposition 187, the law, later struck down by the courts, that killed federal/state funding to undocumented political refugees in the state of California. With its passage, Prop 187 denied school funding to "illegal" (read Latin American) children. The film, Fear and Learning at Hoover Elementary, *was produced by teachers at that school—which has a mostly Latino population, much of it undocumented—and is highly critical of Prop 187, arguing, I think rightly, that its passage was an assault ultimately enacted on the bodies of children. In one particularly disturbing scene, six to seven children are being interviewed about Prop 187, the effects it was having on the school, and their fears now that it was passed. The children are asked if they have ever heard the word "illegal." They nod, slowly. "What does that make you think of?" asks the voice behind the camera. The children each begin to describe how such language makes them feel bad, sad, and wrong. One child, a small, young boy of Mexican descent, says "Dirt. I just feel like dirt." In my mind, I hear Mary Douglas reminding me that dirt is "matter out of place," that dirt is "never a unique, isolated event." Douglas continues, "Where there is dirt there is a system. Dirt is the by-product of a systemic ordering and classification of matter, in so far as ordering involves rejecting inappropriate elements" (35). This child in that video already knows Douglas' work experientially, feeling what it means to be rejected by a system that doesn't want him. And the invisibility of whiteness that makes possible his exclusion, the exclusion of his body, his body of color, does not need to be spoken—it is felt as he partially covers his face, turning slightly from the camera as if to shield himself. Douglas again echoes, "The pullulating person is always in the wrong. He [or she] has developed some wrong condition or simply crossed some line which should not have been crossed and this displacement unleashes danger" (13). It is a displacement that marks this child's body, carving deep wounds that could affect how he will forever see himself. Foucault notes, "In our societies, the systems of punishment are to be situated in a certain 'political economy' of the body: even when they do not make use of violent or bloody punishment, even when they use 'lenient' methods involving confinement or correction, it is always the body that is at issue" (*Discipline* 25). And I see that punishment on the body of this child.*

This moment hurts. But that hurt is compounded when the librarian enters the scene. He seems to have been listening to the children off camera and now he stands over the table. His elderly bald white head gleams in the bright lights. He begins to argue with the children, their fifth-grade eyes watching him as he narrates about the good ol' days when "his" neighborhood was cleaner, less violent. He says something like, "Now, there's trash all over the place—and I'm not saying you all did it," he says pointing to the kids, "but I sure didn't do it." The kids begin to object, noting that they haven't thrown any trash on the streets. "I didn't say ya did, but it wasn't here before," he retorts. One girl, her black hair pulled back in a pony-tail, explains that he did accuse them: "you just said it wasn't here before we Latinos got here and then you said it is here now, suggesting that we are the ones who put it here." In a single sentence, she has deconstructed his entire argument. "You're putting words in my mouth. I'm just saying this neighborhood is falling apart." He says this last part wagging his finger at the children. I always watch this part in horror, thinking about the connection of Latino culture and trash, the connection and explanation of Douglas' theories of dirt, order, power, and systemic process. He is policing them, reminding them of their place-this adult with the power of the institution of schooling behind him, wagging his finger at the children sitting in the brightly colored chairs sized for their young age and small stature. This scene is so violent to me, this man arguing and attacking the children as they sit before him. Power is so clearly defined— when the man fails in argument, he pulls rank, the finger shaking in disapproval.

After the break, my students are eager to talk about the film. They have been murmuring about it for some time in the halls and I have to call them back in for a collective conversation. I try not to lead, but instead ask for places to start our talk. A white woman to my right, her blond hair pulled back in much the same style as the girl in the video, begins. "I thought the video was interesting, but I wanted to just say something about the librarian incident." Okay, I think, here we go. "I was surprised by how disrespectful those kids were. I would have been so offended if students talked to me like that." The man next to her agrees, "That was certainly my first reaction. Kids are so disrespectful these days." The use of "kids" strikes me as interesting—a safe marking of difference that obscures the citation of privilege that makes the critique of these "kids" of color the "problem."

Eventually, the conversation changes; I ask them to consider the power differentials between the librarian and the children—to remember that these were children and to think about how it must have felt to have that white man wagging his finger at them. I ask them to imagine what it means to be so connected to dirt, trash, and excess that the boy so quickly turns to those very images to describe "illegal"—a status he knows and feels personally. On the surface, this conversation is not surprising—it is a way for my mostly white, privileged, middle-class college students to protect themselves. It is a way to remake safety—to rediscipline the bodies of those children in that video so as to avoid the underlying question: How is this classroom, this field of education, the very future careers they are studying for, implicated in the displacement of the children speaking in that video? How does their exclusion (and our continual blaming of them for faults outside of their control or design) perpetuate our own whiteness? In that act, those students remade whiteness just as much as they watched that librarian remake his. Those lines, those marks dug into the flesh of those othered, work to make sure that the unspoken whiteness in that library and in my classroom go unchecked.

The heart of my research focuses on education, working to uncover the body's relationship to the classroom and learning. I have sought to sketch out a vision for multicultural education that truly challenges and breaks down the white cultural center. This work has led me to the classroom as a site of study, working to see how race, the raced body, and racial subjectivities are formed or constituted in educative processes (Hytten and Warren; Warren, "Doing"; Warren, "Performing Whiteness"; Warren and Fassett). While the classroom functions within institutional rules that might restrict the performance of self (McLaren, *Schooling*), I would argue that this site still provides a sense of students' mundane understandings and enactments of race. For example, scholars note the cultural code-switching that students of color must perform in order to succeed in schools (Carger; Delpit; Valdés). Not excluding or ignoring other attributes that may mark difference in ways that otherize students in schools (class, gender, sexuality, etc.), most white students have no such need to hide or perform themselves in any other way than they usually do (based solely in their racial identities). This is to say, if schooling, as Delpit so powerfully makes clear, operates within the culture of power, which is coded with whiteness, then white students who enter schooling need alter their racial performance of self very little to fit into the system of education. In fact, the nature of whiteness as a performative construct that hides its own production means that part of its construction is to make the shift from home to school almost seamless for white subjects. The system of education so institutionalizes the norms of whiteness that entry into schooling for many students of color is an entry into a very different cultural world. Thus, students of color quickly fall into remedial tracks, find themselves subject to disciplinary mechanisms, and attain "at risk" labels.

This chapter details a theoretical framework for seeing the conditions that affect performances of whiteness in educational practice. While the cultural logic behind these performances of whiteness extends far beyond the confines of educational practice, I would suggest that the site of education provides a lens through which to see such productions of raced identities. The framework

I establish below aims to detail the cultural logic behind such performative constructions of whiteness. My central questions are: If whiteness is schooled through embodied and discursive practices, to what end does such a cultural construction get made? What are the cultural values embedded within such an educative production? And further, how does the body in school get conceptualized within the cultural logic of whiteness? If whiteness is a cultural performance that reconstitutes itself, upon what does whiteness rely in such a reproduction?

The Purity of Bodily Absence

There are codes or rules for participating in power; that is, there is a "culture of power." The codes or rules I'm speaking of relate to linguistic forms, communicative strategies, and presentation of self; that is, ways of talking, ways of writing, ways of dressing, and ways of interacting. (Delpit 25, emphasis in original)

In one of the most thought-provoking texts on culture in the classroom, Delpit argues that schooling, like other institutions, is embedded in a culture that regulates, controls, and mediates interaction among participants. This is not a new argument. Peter McLaren, Michelle Fine, Paul Willis, and others have written extensively on how schooling reproduces cultural norms, fulfills cultural expectations, and regulates cultural resistance. In his work in a working-class school system in Toronto, McLaren (*Schooling*) argues that students are continually taught, through symbolic rituals and educative practices, to be good workers and good Catholics. Fine examines urban schools and locates a rhetoric of school failure that continues to blame students for their failure in school without any reflexivity as to the school's own implication in that process. In Willis' classic study, he argues that schooling systematically works to reproduce class structures: for instance, children of the working class continue to be directed in their education, implicitly and explicitly, toward working-class jobs. McLaren's, Fine's, and Willis' works not only examine inequities in schooling, but locate the educational system as being first and foremost intimately involved in the outcomes of these students, in that the school works to perpetuate inequalities rather than resist them. Additional scholarship on identity construction in schools (McCarthy and Crichlow; Rodriguez and Villaverde; Sheets and Hollins; Valdés) supports these initial findings. In particular, Sleeter (1993) argues that, in her experience, traditional teacher education programs "reinforced, rather than reconstructed, how white teachers viewed children of color" (158). In this example, Sleeter demonstrates how schooling reaffirms normalized racist beliefs rather than working to create a progressive teaching force that challenges oppressive ideologies. Each of these studies demonstrates a system or "culture of power" at work making students—making them products of their environment and their social class, all while pointing out how they differ from those who are economically, socially, and culturally successful. Delpit suggests that the rules of the culture of power are a "reflection of the rules of the culture of those who have power" (25). In other words, those who fall outside of the culture of power must learn and participate in the rules of the powerful, for it is the powerful who have made the rules, as well as the game, in the first place.

To begin to articulate how and why this system regulates itself, I return to Mary Douglas' work on cultural purity and contamination, in which she argues that cultural systems work toward maximum control and efficiency by maintaining a smooth and impurity-free systemic flow. In other words, Western culture is invested in hygiene, purity, and order and demands nothing less of our educational system—Douglas' description of dirt, impurities, contaminants, and the like as simply "matter out of place." Thus, dirt is anything that falls outside of the systemic order of things: "Dirt then, is never a unique, isolated event. Where there is dirt there is a system. Dirt is the by-product of a systemic ordering and classification of matter, in so far as ordering involves rejecting inappropriate elements" (35). Douglas provides a keen sense of various cultural systems dependent on cleanliness that are constructed by and structured on relationships—something can only be out of place in relation to something else. Thus, a system is a structure where everything is in line, neat and tidy.

Schools, like many other systems, depend heavily on keeping things neat and tidy. Besides conversations now brewing about school uniforms, dress codes, and other conformity and regulatory ideals, schools promote cleanliness in its most structured form. The entire school day is structured in such a way as to keep the mass of students where they are supposed to be. Students are slotted into hard plastic chairs, shuffled into rows, stacked in levels, and directed toward the front of the room where a teacher stands lecturing "knowledge" to note-taking students. Movement is highly regulated: Bells dictate the beginning and ending of the class session, students must rapidly gather their possessions at the end of the hour and rush to the next subject, teachers stand in the halls to ensure safe and efficient use of "free" time, and so on. Even the ability to use the restroom—the most basic of bodily needs—depends on the student's request, hopefully leading to the willingness of an instructor to allow passage to the restroom, legitimized by a hall pass that narrates permission to be "out of place" when caught by a school official. Schooling, in order to function smoothly, must keep students in their place or risk chaos, a pollution of the orderly flow of things. While this may sound like a cynical view of educational rules, my tone is to suggest that educational practice is a highly structured, clearly marked, and finely ordered system. Schools maintain order by making sure bodies function according to the systemic norms.

The maintenance and regulation of bodies described above does more than focus students' attention on learning; it defines educational activity by demanding that students adhere to a series of arbitrary rules imposed on them by others. However, regardless of the impact these rules and structures have on student learning, the structuring and ordering of education ultimately functions as ideology: It is a reification of an epistemological ordering that places the mental over the material. This means that the educational body must be domesticated in order for the mind to be able to think. Foucault argues that a docile and disciplined body "is the prerequisite of an efficient gesture" (*Discipline* 152). Drew Leder argues that "for Descartes [the mind is], in the strictest sense, nowhere. The mind as immaterial, a substance entirely opposed in nature res extensa, has no extension or location in space" (108). Thus, the mind is free from the potential misrepresentation of bodily sensation. While the power of the mind/body split finds much critique in education literature (see hooks, *Teaching*; McLaren, *Schooling*; and Pineau, "Teaching"), schooling practices consistently work to erase the presence of bodies in educational activity. As McLaren argues: "There was a distinct eros-denying quality about school life, as if students were discarnate beings, unsullied by the taint of living flesh" (221). For, as Leder argues so forcefully, the Cartesian dualistic legacy tells us that "the body [. . .] naturally inclines us to error," while relishing and trusting the "careful mind" (129). Schooling is a process in which the cultural value lies in the mind, while the body should be rendered subsidiary to the cognitive, the immaterial.

At the risk of furthering a personification of "the system" of education, I find it valuable to further extend this analysis with the critical work of Leder, who provides a vocabulary for understanding how the system renders bodies recessive in educational activity in an effort to attend to and concentrate on the mind. Before connecting his work to education, it is vital to understand how Leder conceptualizes bodily absence.

In *The Absent Body*, Leder opens his discussion by distinguishing two kinds of bodily disappearance: focal and background (26–7). Focal disappearance refers to the self-effacement of particular parts of the body when they are used as the location of perceptual experience; but background disappearance, perhaps more suited for the purposes of discussing educational experience, designates a part of the body that falls out of the perceptual field or takes a supportive role. In other words, focal disappearance consists of a shift from the thing felt to the thing feeling. If I feel the tip of my finger, I can feel the fingerprint and any scratches or scars, but when I then use the finger to feel the table in front of me, the finger itself falls into a focal disappearance and becomes the mechanism through which I can feel the table. This differs from background disappearance, which consists more of placing a bodily part in the background. For instance, if I shut my eyes and allow the sound or smell to foreground as my perceptual primary, my eyes recede into a background disappearance—no longer being actively utilized.

While Leder's work on the body clearly focuses more explicitly on the phenomenological body, where the analysis of bodily absence is more firmly centered on the experience of one's own body, I believe he provides a heuristic frame for understanding the body in culture. Where Leder discusses parts of the body receding into a background disappearance, one could adapt his work to account for the way schooling places the body in a background disappearance, where the body is perceptually rendered absent in an effort to center perceptual attention on the mind.

I find that Leder provides an effective frame for understanding the effects of how the Cartesian split plays out in education: The educational body must be rendered absent, forced into a background disappearance. To use Leder's frame of bodily absence and presence, one must account for the problematic Western binary of absence/presence on which he relies, for I would never argue that the body is actually "absent" in schools. However, the metaphor of presence/absence is useful here in that it points to the dramatic effort in schools to erase the impact of the body. Certainly, the body continues to make itself present: Pregnant teen bodies in small desks, overweight bodies in physical education, queer bodies in sexual education, and physically disabled bodies in group activities remind us that bodies are never actually absent. Indeed, Foucault's work on the training and maintenance of docile bodies relies on the physical presence of bodies functioning according to the desire of the system; however, the maintenance of these bodies is in service of a particular end—to make the

bodies function so smoothly as to push them to the background of our perception. Here, Leder argues that the bodies go into a background disappearance—a
state in which bodies are *functionally* absent. Bodies are rendered absent through
their adherence to institutional norms. For these reasons, I maintain Leder's
binary of presence/absence as a conceptual frame, for I think it illuminates the
power of these systems at work on students' physical bodies.

Bringing Leder into conversation with Douglas' notion, I contend that the
purity of the system demands that one keep the body in the background, for the
body, which is always already understood as "matter out of place" in schools,
disrupts their practice and functioning. The smooth functioning of schooling
depends on the absent body, for if the body finds itself present, the system is
contaminated. And if we bring this back to Delpit's original argument that
schools function within a cultural system of those in power, it is the presence of
certain bodies that stand as contaminants within the "normal" functioning of
the system. It is precisely the presence of different bodies—differently abled,
differently colored, differently gendered—that provides the tension within Foucault's theorizing of bodies as docile in systems of power (*Discipline*). It is the
fact that systems encounter resistance that drives them to continually self-
regulate.

The Color of Dirt

> The very terms we use to describe the major ethnic divide presented in Western soci-
> ety, "black" and "white," are imported from and naturalized by other discourses. Thus,
> it is said [. . .] that there are inevitable associations of white with light and therefore
> safety, and black with dark and therefore danger, and that this explains racism [. . .].
> [A]gain, and with more justice, people point to the Judaeo-Christian use of white and
> black to symbolise good and evil, as carried in such expressions as "a black mark,"
> "white magic," "to blacken the character," and so on. (Dyer, "White" 45)

Surely, one could argue, we all enter the classroom as embodied creatures—
one cannot just leave one's body at the door. I feel my body in my desk,
cramped and stiff. I feel my back ache from the hard plastic, figured in various
orthopedic shapes for various sized people. Yet, Leder never suggests that in
background disappearance one loses the body or that this absence is ever literally something that is no longer there. Rather, he argues that the body falls into
the background of one's perception. Disappearance becomes a metaphor for

how bodies are treated in educational systems, effectively erased in an always already unfulfilled desire for absence—a yearning to rid ourselves of our bodily encasements in order to better focus our mental capacities.

While the desire for bodily absence is apparent in Western schooling, not all bodies have the capacity for easy absence—certain bodies are more capable of eluding detection than others. When Delpit discusses the culture of power, she implicitly locates the center of power in white subjects, noting that it is the "black" and/or "lowerclass" student who falls outside that cultural norm upon which the power most assuredly resides (34). Such a conceptualization of race foregrounds how bodies enter educational systems with cultural and social histories inscribed upon them. Race, as Dyer notes, is always available for reading: "Visual culture demands that whites can be seen to be whites" (*White* 44). Whether accurate or not, the reading is always ideological, always based in a historical legacy of race relations. But people do examine bodies, searching for racial identity among other identifying markers, and making conclusions based on the text in front of them, regardless of whether those readings are correct or not.

The metaphorical use of absence, together with convictions by Dyer in the epigraph that opens this section, begins to articulate the power of metaphor as a way of structuring human understanding. For through metaphor, the terms Western culture uses for identifying racial identities carry much ideological weight. As George Lakoff and Mark Johnson argue:

> Human thought processes are largely metaphorical. This is what we mean when we say that the human conceptual system is metaphorically structured and defined. Metaphors as linguistic expressions are possible precisely because there are metaphors in a person's conceptual system. (7)

Lakoff and Johnson provide a conceptual frame from which to understand racial metaphors. Words with metaphorical power like "white" and "black" carry vast ideological weight, as Dyer so powerfully makes clear in the epigraph. Indeed, the symbol of whiteness connotes purity, cleanliness, and goodness, while images of blackness (whiteness's metaphorical opposite) suggest deviancy, evil, and pollution. Whiteness's purity is often connected to absence—whiteness exists without color, free of unnatural substances, in a virginlike state. Color, which must be added, contaminates and exudes excess, a making present of the body. Dyer powerfully articulates this use of metaphor:

> It was a fascinating paradox. Black, which, because you had to add it to paper to make a picture, I had always thought of as a colour, was, it turned out, nothingness, the absence of all colour; whereas white, which looked like just empty space (or blank paper), was, apparently, all the colours there put together. No doubt such explanations of colour have long been outmoded; what interests me is how they manage to touch on the construction of the ethnic categories of black and white in dominant representation. In the realm of categories, black is always marked as a colour (as the term "coloured" egregiously acknowledges), and is always particularizing; whereas white is not anything really, not an identity, not a particularizing quality, because it is everything—white is no colour because it is all colours. ("White" 45)

The ability to be both everything and nothing, always present and always absent, grants whiteness extraordinary cultural power, which helps to structure how we see and understand categories of color.

A key point of interest here is how whiteness as the absence of color gets correlated to the desire in schools for absent bodies. In a cultural system like education which demands that bodies recede into the background, it is easier for the white students, who are always already metaphorically absent (in Leder's sense), as members of the culture of power. While not all races experience equal amounts of discomfort, the student of color enters into the classroom with bodily excess: too much color, too much presence. In Leder's terms, the body of color making itself present in the system suffers from a dys-appearance. The Greek prefix *dys* signifies that body which, due to its appearance in times of illness or error, comes to stand out or is forced into attention: "Dysappearance is a mode, though by no means the only one, through which the body *appears* to explicit awareness" (Leder 86, emphasis in original). The body of color stands out as a mark, a color, a stain upon the fabric on which the schooling system is constituted. Bodies of color, like Dyer's marking on a blank piece of paper, stand out against the expected absence of color. In a system that demands and relies on purity absent of color contaminants, the bodies of color stand out in all their bodily excess. And in that presence, the bodies are effectively dysfunctional—not doing what is expected in a system so heavily reliant on bodily absence.

By marking color upon the cultural expectation of invisible whiteness in education, the dysfunctional body of color functions like dirt in Douglas' conceptual understanding of pure systems. Consider Dyer when he so clearly notes the sanitization of whiteness: "To be white is to have expunged all dirt ... from oneself: to look white is to look clean" ("White" 76). In Douglas' work on purity and systemic sanitation, the body of color, that figure out of place in the cultural system of educational practice, is always in error in education:

> A polluting person is always in the wrong. He [or she] has developed some wrong condition or simply crossed some line which should not have been crossed and this displacement unleashes danger for someone [. . .]. Pollution can be committed intentionally, but intention is irrelevant to its effect—it is more likely to happen inadvertently. (113)

For Douglas, intent to pollute fails to matter. It is simply the contaminant's presence in the system that disrupts the normal functioning of it. The body of color thus fails to perform properly. That body, because of the cultural discursive practices that make color visible and the metaphorical baggage color carries, always already forces attention to itself.

The body of color thus becomes paradoxical in the educational system. The body should be absent, forced so completely into the background that its presence is negligible. In this manner, the body of color strives to fulfill the unfulfillable—it is always already attempting to achieve that which cannot be done, for the body carries too much color, too much excess. Additionally, the presence of the body of color and the fact that it cannot achieve absence is exactly what maintains white privilege. It is exactly the presence of "different" bodies that demands the hierarchy which places whiteness invariably over color, for what could ensure the dominance of whiteness more than the impossibility of the erasure of bodies of color? Thus, the desire for bodily absence works to secure the maximum amount of privilege for whiteness through the continual marking and disciplining of bodies of color—those bodies that are already outside the "normalized" construct of the educational system.

The Maintenance of Order

> With us pollution is a matter of aesthetics, hygiene or etiquette, which only becomes grave in so far as it may create social embarrassment. The sanctions are social sanctions, contempt, ostracism, gossip, perhaps even police action. (Douglas 73)

Briefly, I want to explore how schooling, as an institutionalized space within the culture of power, works to erase those present bodies, reduce impurities in the system, and maintain order. Again, I feel it is important to note that bodies of color are contaminants only because of the cultural, social, and historical understandings of race that render skin pigment as a difference that matters. As Jessie Daniels so powerfully notes in her analysis of white supremacy discourse, which she convincingly argues mirrors mainstream understandings of race, whiteness gets constructed discursively as pure and in need of protecting. On the other hand, nonwhites are constructed as dangers to the security and sanitation of whiteness. But how does schooling account for and respond to these constructions of purity and danger? How does schooling work to create order, filter difference, and maintain the integrity of the system in the face of these breaches of school norms? And how does this, through the mechanisms that work to create stability, demonstrate how schools manage the "dirt" and "bodily excess" in schooling practices?

Schooling, like any organization that finds a threat of contamination, strives to protect itself from that which pollutes it. Many times, these protective mechanisms do not directly appear discriminatory, nor do they seem to target and punish bodies of color in particular. Rather, they take the form of cultural values, methods of learning, styles of interaction, and other educational rituals that continually reinforce the culture of power. From the "founding fathers" to Manifest Destiny, from lectures to quiet time, from capitalism to majority rule, from individualism to behaviorism, education continues to promote the ideals of the culture of power. Those in the culture of power find their values, habits, and styles of interaction promoted and reified in educative practices. Herbert Kohl (1994) details the way schooling systematically works to maintain the culture of power through curriculum and teaching methods. For instance, he describes sitting in a San Antonio classroom in which the instructor is lecturing on "The First People to Settle Texas" (26–7). The students, many of whom are Latino, object immediately as the textbook and the instructor name white settlers from the east as the first occupants of Texas. One student asks, "What are we, animals or something?" The instructor responds by asking in return, "What does that have to do with the text?" In this example, more than bad pedagogy is at play; the issue is the way our curriculum and instructional methods are many times designed not to encourage critical conversations that challenge the white center of power. The question by the teacher is telling—he essentially asks, What does that critique mean in the context of this narrative in this textbook? How does this help students learn what the text is saying? The example sheds light on how those in the culture of power often find their values, habits, and styles of interaction promoted and reified in educative practices. In Kohl's example, the white perspective—the reliance on rote memory, the rhetoric of Manifest Destiny, and the Western ideal of lecture—are all held up as uncritiqueable. On the other hand, the students of color who objected to the content and their lack of voice find themselves in a system not of their own design— they are refused the ability to voice opposition back to the instructor. Here, the students of color are not disciplined via direct punishment, but rather they are reminded that schools function according to particular kinds of rules, rules which remind those in marginalized positions that they are subject to the desires of those in power. In this way, students of color find themselves in a system not of their own design:

> Systems of domination, imperialism, colonialism, and racism actively coerce black folks to internalize negative perceptions of blackness, to be self-hating. Many of us succumb to this. Yet blacks who imitate whites (adopting their values, speech, habits of being, etc.) continue to regard whiteness with suspicion, fear, and even hatred. (hooks, *Killing* 32–3)

Students of color are punished most discretely by being forced into a school system that reinforces the cultural values, styles of interaction, communicative norms, and learning methods valued by the culture of power. If students want to succeed economically or socially, they must comply with the norms of school. Delpit, in her discussion of children of color in white school systems, argues for a balance between learning the codes of power while also finding ways of maintaining identity. While all educational subjects must play by these rules, students of color begin schooling already outside of the culture of power and immediately have a harder struggle for success. They must begin already behind, already forced to code switch. When one adds the myth of meritocracy, which is the illusion of a preestablished equality that is characteristic of the rhetoric of individualism perpetuated by the discursive power of whiteness and education, one comes to believe that we are all equal, thus easily placing blame on those "individuals" who can't make the grade (see Fine; McQuillan; Willis). Students of color, this logic argues, fail not because of a system that continually works against them, but because of their own individual inabilities.

The maintenance of order in schools, those disciplinary efforts to erase color, which clearly fall most significantly on bodies of color, performatively reconstructs white privilege and dominance through the continual marking and reification of racial difference. And while I may risk normalizing blackness and whiteness so much that white children seem to naturally have normed behaviors while children of color do not, these separations are not so cut and dried—they are performative norms, (re)created and reified by subjects. The norms that govern schooling are no more natural than they are necessarily advantageous. Adapting from Butler's work on gender, race "is what is put on, invariably, under constraint, daily and incessantly, with anxiety and pleasure" ("Performative" 282). But it is by maintaining the markers of difference (and the racial/cultural norms reified by schools)that whiteness's strength grows, through its invisibility in a system targeting bodies that fail to properly recede.

Part Two

Repetitive Acts of Purity

Chapter Three

Staged Accomplishments of Whiteness

On performance days in the "Performing Cultures" course, magic happens. From the introductory performances to the final round of group performances, the students produce magic. As I think about writing these performances, I am pulled, drawn, and overwhelmed at the wonder of students doing performance. It is humbling to have had the privilege of bearing witness to people constructing and engaging in issues of culture through the medium of their own bodies. It is a privilege that I do not take lightly. I can't. The stakes are too high. From the first inhalation of breath to the last clapping hand, these constructions make meaning in that room. And together, the teachers, the students, and myself are the subjects of those lessons. It is a kind of magic, those performances. They matter.

As I flip through pages of fieldnotes—rough attempts to capture the magic these students produced—I pause at Janice's personal narrative about being robbed while working in a video store. I remember her curled up in a small ball, her legs pressed tightly against her chest as her pale arms held them. The softness of her voice as she told of "looking in the face of a mugger," this man, this black man, this black man whom she fears will find her again, do it again, hurt her again. I remember how tiny and fragile she looked as she cried. I remember Janice well. I remember feeling the weight of her story, the real terror she must have felt. But I also remember feeling the weight of another person in the room. My fieldnotes don't mention Curtis, but he is there, crystal clear in my memory. Curtis was the only black man in that section of "Performing Cultures." He sat next to me, a baseball cap pulled low over his eyes, those eyes watching the myth getting retold, that myth of violent black men as predators of white women. And while Curtis' body never shifted, never moved during that performance, I could almost see the weight of that marking fall upon his shoulders. And it is Curtis' body that I see as I look at the fieldnotes of that day. While I believe that Janice did not mean to locate her classmate as the object of that performance, I also know intent must have mattered little for Curtis in that moment. The spell had already been cast. And I realized again how much these performances matter. How much effect they have on the minds, bodies, and spirits of those who watch them. For they are pedagogy; they do teach. From the first inhalation of breath, to the last clapping hand, these constructions make meaning. And together, the teachers, the students, and myself were the subjects of those lessons. It is a kind of magic, those performances. They matter. And the privileges that are constructed in the classrooms I witnessed are not constructions that I take lightly. I can't. The stakes are too high.

My ethnographic work has allowed me to witness approximately one hundred and fifty performances, many worthy of lengthy analysis. They vary stylistically, from performances of literature to those of personal narratives, from the performance of nonfiction essays to dramatic scripts written by the students themselves. The performances differ in content: Some are overtly political, on sexuality, racism, AIDS, divorce, and disabilities; while others focus on everyday life, including issues such as the loss of the family dog and growing up on a family farm. Most feature single performers, yet many are constructed by groups of two or more people. The performances derive from three assignments: 1) a performance of a cultural other from the textbook *New Worlds of Literature* (Beaty and Hunter); 2) an intertextual performance asking the students to place together at least two texts (either personal or literary) in order to illuminate a cultural theme; and 3) a group performance that closely examines a cultural group or phenomenon. In the first assignment, students are asked to dramatize a text from the class anthology, in order to come to understand and embody the culture in which the speaker in the text is located. Because the students are working first and foremost from another's words, their task in this assignment becomes one of sifting through the language of the poem or short story to understand that cultural position more clearly. The second assignment is intertextual and is often narrated by students as their favorite because they have more flexibility in the creation of their performances: Students are asked to juxtapose two or more texts on a cultural theme and create a presentation that explores some facet of that theme. They can choose from and build upon one of the following themes, as specified by the anthology: home, family, heritage, language, aliens, fences, crossing, Americans, and beliefs. Many times, students author one or more of the texts, allowing their own experiences to speak back to a writer chosen from the Beaty and Hunter collection. These performances are less about the discrete texts themselves and more about how a performer might put texts together to make an argument about a cultural issue. The final round consists of group performances that explore a cultural group or phenomenon. In these performances, students work together in teams of three to six members to research and construct a presentation that attempts to give an accurate account of a given cultural group or issue. These teams of students examine culture in the broadest sense.

Here, I critically read students in staged performance. This is a potentially tricky business for, as a scholar of performance, I have become a rather competent reader of the nuances of this kind of work. The students I am reading, however, are not. They are undergraduate students, many of whom are taking their first performance class. Often, the students do not have the kind of deliberate awareness regarding performance choices and their implications that my analysis might suggest. In addition, my reading may or may not match the experiences of the other students in the class, who may not see, or read, the same kinds of implications from these representations. In order to account for this, I make great efforts here to avoid psychologizing my fellow audience members or to try to anticipate the thoughts or intentions behind the performer as I read these performances. I do so for two key reasons. First, I just can't know how everyone might read a given set of performances, nor do I think that asking them necessarily provides the information for which I am looking. I find the students' own admissions less informative than an examination of what the performances themselves accomplish. Therefore, my reading of the performances moves from their experiences to my own dialogue with how these presentations work to maintain the dominance of white cultural privilege.

Second, I am not interested in intent. As Timothy Gould forcefully notes, there is a "perlocutionary delay" between one's illocutionary utterance (intent) and the ultimate perlocutionary effect (result) (31). Put another way, just because one does not intend to oppress others with an utterance or nonverbal expression does not mean that s/he is not responsible for the effects such communicative messages might have on others. If one reduces racism to intent, then whiteness is again protected through white talk; white folks hold no responsibility for the perpetuation of racism and therefore they are free to keep inequities in place through their own inaction. I find it vital to move away from intent and focus on these performances as texts made available for public consumption and critical analysis. Certainly, performers' motivations may vary. They might be speaking from limited performance experience, trauma, or few life experiences with cultural others. For this reason, I am not presuming to account for *why* they are saying and doing what I see before me. Rather, I am interested in the performances as texts that are offered up for critical interrogation as meaningful citations or repetitions of familiar cultural scripts. I am interested in *how these performances function*, not the message the performer intended for his/her audience.

In the classrooms I witnessed, students performatively constructed whiteness in four overlapping, yet individually significant, ways. Each of these patterns works strategically to constitute whiteness as a protected identity embedded in and embodying the maintenance of pure systems of privilege. First, students worked to erase differences, constructing sameness at the expense of any cultural discrepancy. Second, students often constructed contradictions in their performances that undermined the rhetorical impact of their performance text. Third, students relied on stereotypical understandings of people, protecting whiteness through misleading or grossly simplistic representations of others. Fourth, students called upon the rhetoric of victimhood, locating themselves as the victims of racist systems and thus occupying the positions of both dominator and oppressed simultaneously. I noted these themes as I sifted through my fieldnotes, working to find a schema that matched the kinds of patterns I was noticing in the classroom performances. Thus, each of these themes represents a way of making sense of how I experienced these public cultural representations.

Constructing Sameness:
"It doesn't matter what our differences are!"

When discussing issues of race and difference, several of the students in each of the classes I observed relied on a rhetoric of similarity or sameness, which worked to erase the power of difference. Often these elisions were constructed as antiracist, where the denial of difference is offered as a mechanism to create a more peaceful coexistence in which individuals focus on cultural similarities to the exclusion of difference. This strategy relies on notions of color blindness, creating an illusion of preestablished racial equality (Dyer, *White*; Frankenberg; Thompson). The performatives of this type boil down to a familiar cultural logic: if we are really the same, then race doesn't matter. Certainly, this way of thinking has been deconstructed by many scholars, most significantly in whiteness literature by Ruth Frankenberg, who argues that such erasures of color are an exercise of "power evasion" in that the power behind race is ignored, securing white privilege through invisibility (14).

To begin this discussion, I turn to several variations of color evasion in which difference is elided in an effort to focus attention on sameness. Mary, a young white-appearing woman with long brown hair, sits on the corner of the large metal desk wearing an oversized T-shirt bearing Looney Tunes characters. Her voice is high pitched, suggesting stereotypical childlike youthfulness as she does this autobiographical narrative from her childhood. Mary describes growing up with Patty, the "Mexican girl next door":

There are differences. She plays Mexican music and I like piano. I say "dad," she says "papa." *She is spoiled—I'm not!* But our differences *aren't color*, but in what we do. [...] Her family painted their house bright blue. Even Patty realized how *strange* that was! Our families were different, but Patty *and I are really the same*. We like the same things. *It doesn't matter what our differences are!* (my emphases)

As Mary finishes her piece, she smiles, nods her head, and returns to her seat.

I begin with Mary's performance because it highlights the most obvious way that whiteness gets enacted through the performative citation of sameness. Mary narrates a rather simple relationship from her childhood, drawing on her friendship with Patty to serve as a symbol of possible interracial relationships. Under the intertextual theme of "crossing," Mary highlights the ways that similarity bridges difference, yet the bridge here is constructed at the expense of that which is crossed—the differences between Mary and Patty. Obscuring this difference is significant; it renders cultural difference as equatable with musical taste and terms of endearment toward their fathers. In fact, even the judgment of Patty's home being painted bright blue as "strange" is constructed as a shared critique that places Patty's Mexican family as abnormal, protecting the normalcy of Mary's own whiteness. Yet even if Patty and Mary both vocalize a critique of the blue paint, they probably do so for different reasons. While Mary may rely on her normative values embedded in whiteness, Patty's accounting for the strangeness of the choice of paint may be a protection strategy. That is, Patty may recognize the precarious nature of her position as outside normative whiteness and therefore agrees that the choice is strange in order to preserve her sense of self. That is, while Mary's speech is a performative of white privilege that ensures her own normativity and dominance, Patty's agreement may be a performative of self-preservation in the face of cultural critique. While we may never know the reason for Patty's agreement, the fact that the question of why one might agree about the strangeness of bright blue paint is never raised functions as a display (and reiteration) of whiteness's power. Thus, as Douglas might suggest, Mary's elision of the cultural differences between her and Patty ensures that the smooth functioning of the system of whiteness goes on cleanly and without challenge.

The trope of sameness functioned in nonwhite identified student performances as well. In an introductory personal narrative performance, a young self-described black man introduces himself to the class through the persona of his army sergeant. Taking on the role of his superior, Leon puffs out his chest and belts: "You have to have faith in the system, Leon! There's no conspiracy against you." In this performance, Leon describes his slow acceptance that he is just like everyone else and must work hard to get what he wants. Juxtaposed to Leon's performance, Robert also details his own cultural experience as an Arab American:[1] "We are still Americans. We should look at people for who they are." Each of these performances, on one level, functions performatively in the same way as Mary's, regardless of the nonwhite identity of the speaker. Leon chose his performance as the way he wanted the class to meet him, as an introduction to "who he was." Robert's strong defense of the belief that everyone will be treated the same regardless of race, that he is "American" too, is a powerful reiteration of color blindness, which is further authenticated by both his and Leon's claim to nonwhiteness (Frankenberg; Thompson). By citing themselves as nonwhite (i.e., Leon's self-description; Robert's claim to Middle Eastern origins), the citation of sameness is coded with authority, for if a person who is traditionally conceived of as oppressed erases difference, it can be seen as a more valid account. After all, why would an oppressed person deny his/her own social position? The citation of sameness here functions to make stable the systemic reproduction of white centrality. However, this citation needs another level of analysis which stems from the speakers' own cultural situatedness. In other words, how might the statements from these students of color serve to performatively locate themselves within the majority so as to protect their own bodies and spirits during the course of the class? It would be easy to say that these students are just judgmental dopes under the hegemonic hypnosis of mainstream white culture, but it is more complicated to see how these citations are strategic efforts toward cultural survival.

While the above performances served to preserve whiteness by claiming sameness, Josh and Angie constructed an outright denial of difference by mocking the very construction of difference itself. In a performance written by themselves focusing on interracial dating and investigating the theme of "crossing," Josh and Angie reify whiteness in several ways. As Angie tells of dating an African American man, Josh argues back that: "You can't date him, he's not your type! He's black!" Angie smiles and returns, "Listen to them! I like hearing them talk. How can *you* understand someone from a different culture?" The performers continue until Angie breaks out of her dramatic character and steps forward to address the audience directly: "I once had a relationship with a guy named Kevin. He was a black man. Black, white, green, purple—if I like him, I'll date him." Josh moves forward: "I think we are prejudiced because we are scared." The remainder of the performance urges people to embrace interracial relationships, ending with Josh noting that "it's up to us—things will get better if we do."

Whiteness gets constituted in several ways here. First, both performers suggest that they are white through negation. That is, neither identify themselves as white, but rather rely on the unspoken nature of race to create an assumption of whiteness. By constructing self through negation, Josh and Angie reinstitute the cultural power of whiteness by never naming their own identities—they name only what they are not. As Thomas K. Nakayama and Robert L. Krizek make clear, the strategy to not name color is a citation of purity: "The unstated, silenced implication, given its meaning and power from historical usage, is that white means not having any other 'blood lines' to make it impure" (299). Thus, the negative definition is a performative of white purity, necessitating only those who are not so "clean" to use a color label.

Additionally, the power of whiteness as unnamed is compounded when Angie says, "Black, white, green, purple—if I like him, I'll date him." When Angie says this, she not only equates different races and elides power differentials, but also mixes "real" racial constructions with the fictional colors of green and purple. By equating the power of blackness and whiteness with these other colors, racial difference is mocked, rendered a silly comparison that has no weight, no significance. By making such a comparison, whiteness and blackness, as well as the historical and cultural power differentials involved in such identities, are performatively erased or rendered so minimal that it ceases to matter.

While working in a slightly different mode, Marty addresses many of the same concerns in her intertextual collage performance, in which she attempts to examine the very notion of difference itself. In a complex performance, Marty, a white-appearing student, brings together several texts to highlight some of the differences people construct between themselves and others. A personal narrative about her and a man with "dark Mexican eyes" shifts into Robert Frost's "Mending Wall." Marty bends to the floor where she has several apples and a small pile of pine cones separated by a line of loose rocks. She picks up an apple and a pine cone, shifting texts in a transition line: "He's all pine and I'm apple." She places the apple and pine cone on opposite sides of the rock wall so that the apple rests on pine cones and the pine cone is beside the apples; she then tosses a cloth over the entire display. Marty climbs to the top of a large metal desk and recites a monologue from *Romeo and Juliet* on the differences between the rival families. As each piece comes and goes, the speaker's frustration with difference and separation grows in intensity. Finally, she looks to the audience and concludes by asking why we "let differences keep people away from each other? We aren't as different as we may think."

Marty's performance has several layers, each reflecting a complex mix of texts that builds to the ultimate question pondering the use and insistence of difference in our lives. Marty's initial compellation is sophisticated, working to explore how difference has been used to separate people. Her choice of *Romeo and Juliet* following the Frost poem reads as an interesting indictment of the ways separation often wreaks violence on the bodies of those who are affected by that difference—the star-crossed lovers' familial difference is what ultimately leads to their early and tragic deaths. So in many ways, the performance examines the cost of looking only at the discrepancies (metaphorical walls, family differences, etc.) without consideration for how those might be balanced with similarity (shared goals, peace, Romeo and Juliet's transcendent love). Yet, what then becomes interesting is the way the ending question undermines the messages offered in the previous texts she has just narrated. The differences articulated in Frost's "Mending Wall" matter just as the family differences between Romeo and Juliet are of great consequence. This is not to say that Marty's only choice here is to deny the possibility of people coming together from divergent locations. Rather, it is to ask what such a trumping of differences in favor of easy resolutions accomplishes in that performative moment. Marty, in this example, does not maintain the complexity of what it means to be pine cone while another is apple; instead, she undermines those differences by suggesting that "we aren't as different as we think." In an almost parental reminder, Marty notes that the differences are in "our" head, that they are not as real or as consequential as "we" might believe. She displaces complexity and tension by reversing speakers and situations offered in the texts—whiteness gets reiterated, meaningful difference is again replaced with a too simplistic argument for similarity.

In a slightly different manifestation of maintaining whiteness through sameness, Jerry offers a complex enactment of difference through the embodiment (or not) of cultural others. Jerry, a white-appearing performer, created a complicated set consisting of a platform with chairs on either side.[2] As the performance begins, Jerry stands in the center of the platform with an opening narrative from the textbook, making references to growing up black in a white world—a "survivor" of racism. When this first narrative finishes, he walks straight out, looks at the audience, and loudly states, "Fuck Jim Crow, fuck racism!" He then turns and crosses to the empty seat to the left of the platform.

The next piece Jerry performs centers on a young girl being relocated to a Japanese internment camp. While Jerry's tone of voice shifts slightly to accommodate the youthful speaker, he retains his southern accent, his posture only slightly changed. After a few moments in this narrative, he rises, repeats "Fuck Jim Crow, fuck racism!" and proceeds to the chair just right of the platform. There, he sits with his legs wide open, rocking the chair back on its two hind legs. With a thick southern drawl, he begins to address the audience, telling stories about his life with the Ku Klux Klan. As this character talks, Jerry slumps in his chair, his eyes wide, his speech slow, and his expression empty as he describes a person of color, "This one, he's a coon!" When finished, he again utters the connecting line, turns toward the audience, and asks us to consider the destructive power of racism.

There are two key aspects of Jerry's performance that need to be drawn out. First, Jerry's performance is clearly strategic—he took great time to work these pieces together, each following a similar theme, similar narrative styles, and recurring images. His blocking and use of space also suggests care and attention to detail, each strategically crafted to communicate this critique of racism. However, a key aspect of the performance was not marked as clearly as most other choices. While Jerry allows the texts to differentiate the race of the speaker, he fails to mark the presence of another race in vocal tone or posture. While each of the different narrators exhibits subtle differences in volume, mood, or tone that suggest a different speaker, Jerry does not mark racial difference bodily. In fact, none of the characters are marked as racially different except through the language in the script—each narrator is presented in Jerry's own dialect, each embodied in Jerry's general posture and walk such that the performance of each is strikingly similar to Jerry's everyday class behavior. The absence of marking cultural others performatively is significant here. I am not critiquing Jerry for his lack of stage experience, which may account for this lack of character embodiment: I am interested in the way these performative gaps position the narrators being presented. The identical posture and speech in each scene constructs similarity among narrators, regardless of how they are intended by Jerry. Additionally, when Jerry's attention to detail in script and staging is juxtaposed to the lack of marking racial or cultural difference, he only continues to obscure how these narrators and their accompanying life histories are different. Thus, race becomes so unmarked in this performance that the people he performs are essentially unraced—they are "just" human, each telling his individual tale. This elision of race marks invisibility through its absence; that is, the personae are all seemingly white, like Jerry himself.

This omission of race might seem inconsequential except for the fact that Jerry chooses to mark the southern origins and intelligence of the KKK member. As soon as he increases the southern drawl, stupefies the language, and slumps the posture of the white KKK member, he physically and vocally "others" that figure from the rest of the narrators we have met thus far. The performer creates a characterization of the racist—the one we can easily see to be prejudiced. This marking allows Jerry to perform whiteness while not performing self, even if he himself is white. By aligning his everyday performance of self with the nonwhite narrators, he erases their racial difference in and through his own whiteness. Jerry must create another kind of whiteness—an overtly "racist" whiteness coded through dialect, posture, and expression—in order to separate himself from the KKK example he performs. Jerry must cite or locate another, easily recognizable performance of racism, concomitantly deflecting his own in the process. If only overtly racist whiteness gets constituted as different in this performance, it would appear that all of the others are "really the same." The extreme effort to otherize the KKK member deflects Jerry's own associations with whiteness and systems of domination. The presence of this white man's body on stage with the unmarked racial others continues to make whiteness unmarked and uncritiqued, and thus re-creates it as the stable and invisible cultural marker by which all other racial identities, including the overtly racist white person, are measured. Note here how whiteness gets performatively reconstituted: Jerry's othering of the KKK member's whiteness reifies the illusion that racism exists only in the extreme and that Jerry, by aligning himself with physically nonmarked but nevertheless of-color speakers, assumes the role of the nonracist white. His performance of whiteness (re)constitutes racism only as an extreme act of hatred, while the cultural uniqueness of people of color are effectively erased and the speakers conflated with Jerry's own whiteness. Color blindness as a performative of white privilege functions here as a repetitious elision of power differentials that cites the discursive power of meritocracy— the myth that color has no historical legacy of racial inequality (Butler, *Excitable*).

If one places Jerry's performance in dialogue with Sandra's, race gets positioned in a very different way. Sandra, a self-identified African American woman, performs a piece about being biracial. The first segment of her performance is about several persons of racially mixed heritages, detailing their family lines and how they prefer to be addressed. When this segment has concluded, she addresses the audience directly, noting how race is a performance in and of itself, both white and black. She then smiles and states, "And I play," moving to the left of the performance space. Here, her body stiffens and her English becomes standard American. The performance takes on an aristocratic tone as she "smooches" an imaginary other on the cheek in greeting, waving a flowing scarf. After Sandra discusses going out on her yacht, her body returns to its previous posture as she moves center stage, again saying "And I play." As she continues moving stage right, her tone, walk, and language shift. Hand gestures grow larger as the woman speaks in black vernacular about her lack of cash: "Hey, what's up? You know I ain't got no mon-ey!" As Sandra speaks, the language is highly articulated and emotionally charged as she vocally pounds each syllable out in a rhythmic beat.

In the text of Sandra's performance, race is as much an issue as it is in Jerry's, yet here, race gets marked in different ways. Rather than evading the issue of difference, the performance of race itself is taken up as an aesthetic and rhetorical strategy. The performances of whiteness and blackness in amplified stereotypical dimensions function here, ironically, to subvert actual racial identities. While Jerry's decision to distance and separate himself from race seems evident by his appeal to individualism and sameness, Sandra's presentation foregrounds social differences, allowing her to articulate a very different understanding of how racial identity is made through the embodiment of cultural messages, as well as to offer a vision of how one might make race meaningful through a staged performance of identity. Sandra's performance interrupts the everyday performance of race by calling attention to its performative nature—race is allowed to be seen as a social construct, a socially informed performance. It also seems worth noting that this performance is by a woman of color, a woman who has to notice race because this performance of identity has consequences for her in the world. The fact that Jerry can choose not to mark these choices in the performance is made possible only by the privilege of his own whiteness. While Jerry's public message seems to construct antiracism, his underlying message, made possible by a legacy of whiteness and racism, performatively works to remake his privileged position (Scott). But Sandra's performance dramatically works against Jerry's logic. By both highlighting the constructedness of racial categories through her stereotypical enactments and then framing them with "And I play," Sandra undermines the stability of race categories themselves. Thus, the very fact that Jerry can choose whether or not to mark race is a product of white privilege that Sandra's performance takes away, for Sandra cannot assume the same kind of racial invisibility.

The performances in this section each construct sameness between races, yet many do so in ways that performatively work to reinforce racist ideologies, protecting and securing whiteness as the racial center. It is a powerful rhetoric, reiterating a common view of equality regardless of cultural differences. The fact that such performances are framed and, quite possibly, intended to bring people together ignores the missing element: The question remains, to what end does such a construction get made? The performances that continue to rely on simplistic conceptions of sameness without regard for the complexity of difference serve to, as Douglas suggested, preserve the purity of the system. It is an erasure of difference in service of order and the maintenance of racial inequalities. These performances work to erase the danger that difference represents, and they do so by maintaining a system in which white privilege and systemic racism continue unmarked and unchallenged.

Constructing Contradictions: "And then, on *Who Wants to Be a Millionaire?* there was a white man who won $32,000 and he had a girlfriend who was black."

Most often, students begin by narrating a thesis to their performance, asking the audience to focus on a particular rhetorical end in their work. These rhetorical suggestions either occur in the performance itself or are offered afterward in the postperformance discussions. However, many times something happens in the construction of the performance or in the presentation that alters how we see the rhetorical message, creating contradictions or awkward moments when two or more competing factors rub against each other in ways that undermine the intended outcome. In this second pattern of performance themes, I am interested in uncovering how contradictions within a given performance work to negate or deny the intended rhetoric of the piece. In other words, how does an underlying or hidden message work to counter or reverse the overt or explicit message?

A key contradiction in several performances occurred when the speaker advocated antiracism, yet did so within a logic of radical individualism. For example, consider Carrie's intertextual performance on interracial dating, in which she mixed personal narrative with published work by others. The lights have been dimmed in the performance space. Renee, the instructor, gives the ready signal to the performer and music blares from a portable stereo: "Free your mind and the rest will follow," claims the voice. Carrie, a young white woman, enters the room as the music volume is brought down. "A racist: Someone who looks at another and judges them based on skin tone," she begins. From here, Carrie begins to discuss the dangers of racism, speaking directly to the audience.

Through the popular song by En Vogue, Carrie urges the audience to "free their minds" and accept those who choose to date individuals from other racial groups. What is interesting here is that Carrie conflates racism and prejudice, describing the ills of judging someone else "based solely on the color of their skin". Certainly, the term "racist" is often used to signal prejudicial acts, yet the continual connection of individualized acts with the maintenance of racism severely limits the complexity of racial inequality. Racism is more accurately defined as a system of domination, functioning as a system that is enacted through everyone but not localized in any individual (Foucault, *Power/Knowledge*). Prejudices, on the other hand, are those individual acts based on some arbitrary, though historically significant, characteristic (McIntosh). The reduction of racism to individualized actions creates an illusion that changing specific acts would make someone (and society at large) nonracist. As Butler might argue, such a move divorces the historical power of the performative, reducing the act to only discrete localized actions (*Excitable*). While Carrie's performance attempts to work against racist ideologies, she ultimately reifies whiteness by locating systemic oppression in individual actions. This kind of contradiction within the performance undermines Carrie's overt political message, reinforcing the very thing she claims to be deconstructing. The appeal to individualism is a performative—a citation, and concomitantly a reiteration, of whiteness's discursive power, where institutional racism is obscured in order to reinforce white privilege through invisibility.

While the logic of the individual can serve to make people unaccountable for their actions, the complete denial of the individual also contributes to the perpetuation of whiteness through contradiction. For instance, Ellen's performance on interracial dating and marriage strategically works to erase her own agency in relation to racism, in which her efforts to construct improvement are undermined by a separation from the problem. In a very "proper" and formal public presentation, Ellen, who self-identifies as white, offers several examples of how far we've come in terms of race relations, noting how Disney productions were all white until recently, when they've "branched out and started accepting other kinds of people." Then she notes that "the other day I was watching television [. . .] and then, on *Who Wants to Be a Millionaire?* there was a white man who won $32,000 and he had a girlfriend who was black." Behind Ellen, photographs and images from magazines of pale-looking people coupled with people of color serve as the backdrop for her narrative of social progress.

The kind of progress narrative Ellen presents here displaces any need for further action, distancing the speaker from recognizing her own participation in racism (McIntyre). It constructs the problem of racism as getting better, and through that construction whiteness is not only removed from Ellen individually, but is protected from interrogation, since progress is being made. It is as if progress happens outside of the individual and the context from which she speaks; as if, on its own, progress will inevitably lead to social change. Additionally, these progress narratives are problematic, because as Richardson and Villenas note, they still rely on white Western conceptions of the way the world should be. This construction measures the advancements of nonwhites based on the status of whites, performatively constructing whiteness as an identity that needs no attention, no criticism, no change. The progress narrative, as it is constructed in Ellen's performance, creates a contradiction: a celebration of advancement that actually argues the opposite by locating herself (and this class) outside of the discourse of racial inequality. This contradiction renders whiteness and systemic racism uncritiqued.

Ellen's argument of progress can be seen working more subtly in Tom's performance of "Next Life, I'll Be White" by Laurence Thomas. Tom is a very skinny, pale young man. He wears a dark black T-shirt untucked, hanging over faded jeans. In this narrative, the speaker is describing life as a black man and the battles he encounters based on skin tone, noting that if he had the choice to do it again, he would rather not have those constant struggles. Tom constructs a sarcastic speaker who smiles and speaks directly to the audience, stirring up much laughter in the room. Tom finishes the piece two paragraphs before the end of Thomas' essay, concluding:

> I intend to go on living morally as best I can. But it sure would be nice to enjoy on a much more frequent basis one of the benefits that come with living morally—namely, the public trust. And this I would most certainly do if I were white. (Thomas 580)

As he closes, the audience claps. He smiles as he walks back to his seat, noting, "I ended the piece there 'cause I don't like how Thomas does. My ending has a more dramatic effect." He smiles and leans back in his seat. The ending Tom chose not to include is not incidental—it matters. It reconfigures the whole narrative in that it is the closing paragraph that moves from Thomas' personal experience to an indictment of society: "As is the case so often with oppression, the victims are made to feel inadequate for insisting upon what their oppressors enjoy and routinely take for granted" (580).

What I find important in this performance is Tom's trumping of Thomas' voice in order to create a more "dramatic" effect. Thomas' narrative has many twists and turns, ultimately leading to his central point that life as a black man is a life of constant oppressive struggle. Tom's choice to exclude the final narrative line in Thomas' piece clearly alters the rhetorical effect of the work as a whole by reducing the systemic problems Thomas is detailing to a personalized desire to be white. While I appreciate the agency of the performer to make the performance his/her own through textual adaptation, I must ask what gave this performer the permission to argue that his ending should be valued (or at least presented for the audience) as better than Thomas'. It is the negative value placed on Thomas' ending and Tom's assumption that he can make it better that establishes the contradiction for me. Only a white speaker could negate the power of racism that drives Thomas' narrative.

Thus far, performative contradictions have arisen when a speaker advocated one political or ideological position and simultaneously undermined that position through different citations or appeals to whiteness. Other kinds of contradictions are much more subtle, much more difficult to explicate, for the tension lies between the content or rhetorical intent of a performance and the student's physicalization of that text. These readings are complicated by the fact that the students in "Performing Cultures" are often novices, and their characterization skills may vary. I am not advocating a representational style of performance that tries to "replicate" cultural types. Rather, I am asking questions about what happens when the textual content bumps sharply against the visual, when the piece says one thing and the visual appears to say something else. For instance, in a performance of Pocahontas, Laurie, a white-appearing student, begins by noting that her piece is not like the Disney version which "was not accurate." Then, she pulls out a large colorful blanket and drapes it over her shoulders; her long straight blond hair falls on the blanket as she commences with her piece. As she performs, she uses large sweeping gestures; a large voice belts out the lines. My reading of this performance is complicated. First, I do not want to say that Laurie can't perform this piece; I do not want to fall into

Dwight Conquergood's trap of the Skeptic's Cop-out ("Performing"), but I do want to ask what happens when she begins her piece by critiquing Disney's version of Pocahontas and then proceeds to whitewash this Native American speaker. Laurie's blond hair, so pronounced on the bright colors of the blanket, her large dramatic gestures, and powerful voice seem to be at odds with the narrative that Pocahontas tells in this moment. This performance of self communicates a white version of strength that is enacted through strong and dynamic vocals and large sweeping gestures. Additionally, the blond hair so visible on the blanket is a constant reminder of the white Western symbol of beauty. The fact that this image is present for us is a visual contradiction—a performative that reinscribes the ideal of white beauty. Again, while I don't want to ever suggest that Laurie couldn't have pulled this off, I do want to say that every aspect of that performance matters—that every tone, every choice, and every image constructs a performative, rhetorical message for the audience. The fact of that hair, as innocent as it might be, matters as a reproduction of whiteness's centrality.

These kinds of contradictions occurred often. In a performance of "Hard Rock Returns to Prison from the Hospital for the Criminally Insane" by Etheridge Knight, Scott enters the performance space wearing Tommy Hilfiger blue jeans and a T-shirt bearing the name of a popular men's clothing store. He introduces the piece, pulling out a shot glass bearing the logo of his fraternity: "Pretend this is a shot glass full of whiskey." Images of privilege are literally littered through this performance: Scott has a nicely trimmed haircut, his clothes are expensive and sport the biggest names in fashion, and his shot glass connects him to not only university life but the specific site of fraternities. The juxtaposition of these images of economic privilege and the narrative character in the piece, who is clearly a current or former prison inmate, are striking. This is similar to Denny's performance of "Escape the Ghettos of New York" by Vanessa Howard, in which Denny, a white-appearing man, sits in the corner of the room under dim lights holding an empty bottle of tequila. Denny performs the narrator as drunk and homeless, trapped on the streets of New York City. While he sits in the corner, the bottle of alcohol and the random pieces of newspaper upon which he sits are belied by his clothing choices as well. He wears a stylish Nautica polo, cleanly pressed and tucked into his blue jeans. His hair appears highly groomed and his brown leather shoes look relatively new.

While both Scott's and Denny's performance choices can be understood in the context of an introductory performance studies course at a Midwestern university, I contend that such choices matter to the audience who views the performance. The fact of these choices and the contradictions they embody affect how I read the performance; they are contradictions that cause effects. What happens performatively when I witness the repetitions of privilege in the context of narratives of oppression? What does it mean for Mora, an Indian woman performing "Say Hello to John" by Sherley Anne Williams, to juxtapose Williams' narrative, written in black vernacular, to the performance choice of holding a white Cabbage Patch doll in her arms? How does the Cabbage Patch doll, so familiar as a popular representation of privilege, dramatically alter the rhetorical impact of the poem? This contradiction functions as a subtle and insidious repetition of privilege, one more citing of white normativity.

Similarly, Andrew's performance of "Red Anger" by R. T. Smith stands as an interesting example of what happens when contradictory messages arise in the performance. Andrew, a self-identified white student, turns off all the lights in the room and sits behind a large metal table quietly reciting the poem. His voice is almost a monotone, narrating the hard and sometimes hopeless life of this Native American speaker. In the middle of the piece, he screams, flipping the large metal table into the air. The audience reacts, some gasping in excitement as the table lands with the sound of twisting metal. The room is silent as Andrew paces, breathing audibly. The tension is great, building to the next line ... then Andrew begins to laugh: "I just forgot my line." At this, the class laughs loudly. Contradiction is constructed here through the lost line and the juxtaposition of this dramatic expression of anger and the giggling humor with which Andrew follows it. In one stroke, Andrew undermines not only the performance choice of the table flip, but the anger he is trying to capture in this Native American speaker.

Andrew is a fascinating figure in this study, for, like none of the other performances, each of his pieces expresses a contradiction that works to undermine the cultural other he is representing, all while reinforcing whiteness's dominance. In particular, Andrew participated in the semester's ultimate example of protecting whiteness as a privileged construction. He and his girlfriend, Carla, both of whom identify in this performance as white, perform "Say Yes" by Tobias Wolff, in which two married white speakers are discussing whether they would be together if one of them were black. Carla's speaker relies on the logic that love is color-blind, trying to get Andrew's character to say that he would have married her if she had been black. Andrew's character in the short story argues that he would never have gone out with her if she had been black, noting: "You're not [Black], so let's drop it." The short story, however, is interrupted by personal narratives in which Carla and Andrew explain their family histories and how that has marked their understandings of race. Carla notes that she is struggling to undo the racism implanted by her father, while Andrew was raised "not to look at skin color but in their heart." While the pieces of the performance have worked nicely to highlight struggle with race and the possibility of interracial partnerships, Andrew ends the piece by asking Carla to come over to him. She does, he kneels and proposes to her. Carla says yes and the room explodes in applause, as this bit of "real life" performance intervenes in the staged drama.

This performance is highly political and internally contradictory. Textually it works to promote the possibility that love is blind and can lead to interracial marriage. However, the proposal by a white man to a white woman at the end of the performance, as well as the audience's enthusiastic sanction of this proposal, only serves to dramatically undermine the very message the rest of the performance strives to create. Thus, with the proposal comes the reiteration of white purity and the maintenance of white heterosexual marriage as the ideal, the only realization of marriage we ever get to see in the performance.

The contradictions in the previous performances were damaging because they were not allowed to be heuristic possibilities for inquiry. An alternative orientation to contradiction is provided by Shelly, a young self-identified white student, whose performance locates contradiction as the location for critique. Shelly tells the class about an article she read in which several people on campus were interviewed to find out if racism was present at this university: "In a survey, a middle-aged black person said 'I have never experienced so much racism as here at this university.'" Shelly notes that she "had no idea that racism was so present here—I have never experienced any problems here. It really affected me that this was the worst racism he ever felt." Certainly, Shelly could have either dismissed the report or just juxtaposed her experience with that of the black man in the interview, both of which would have elevated her at the expense of the interviewee. However, by trying to place his comment in the context of her life, reflecting that she has never had the same experience, Shelly allows that contradiction between his experience and hers to move toward understanding her own cultural privilege. By reflecting on her own position as a white person, Shelly made that contradiction a meaningful site of critical self-reflection.

The performances represented here are just samples of how contradictions can performatively constitute whiteness by reinforcing or protecting whiteness's centrality. It is significant that these performers probably never intended for these messages to work so strategically, but inasmuch as these performances were presented with these rhetorical contradictions, the ideology of whiteness was maintained, reflecting the powerful ways the system of racial privilege exerts itself.

Constructing Stereotypes:
"The face of a mugger"

When McIntosh lists individual privileges that she receives based on her whiteness, she notes that people of color many times serve as stereotypes, while whites are constructed as individuals free from such collective generalizations. In other words, whiteness provides the privilege of being seen as an individual, while nonwhites fall victim to stereotypical constructions based on assumptions of race. In the classroom performances, stereotypes were employed not only as representations of people of color, but also in situations in which the white performer wanted to distance himself/herself from others of his/her race. In either case, the appeal to stereotypes gives white students the ability to disavow some "other" from themselves, thus remaking their own whiteness as not-of-color and simultaneously not-racist.

For instance, I return to Jerry's performance of the KKK member, in which his voice shifted into an exaggerated southern dialect. The southern coding, most notable when the character said "Boy!" dramatically at the beginning of a sentence, relied on stereotypical images of KKK members. By relying on the common perceptions of the racist south, Jerry repeated that stereotype rather uncritically. This appeal to KKK stereotypes allowed Jerry another form of whiteness to rely on as an example of racism. The use of vocals to establish an "other" was embodied in several pieces. Mora, in her performance of "Say Hello to John," spoke the lines of Sherley Anne Williams' poem in black vernacular speech because the text is written to foreground that style of speaking. I am interested, however, in the ways these vocal attributes worked in some cases to reinscribe whiteness's dominance.

In another performance of Smith's "Red Anger," Kenneth, a white-appearing student, chooses to include historical facts about Native American tribes in order to give his audience a context for understanding the narrator of the piece. When Kenneth narrates the historical points, he speaks in his everyday voice, yet, when performing the male Native American speaker, he uses very choppy staccato-like vocals, ending with, "People die very much." Thus, whenever he embodies the Native American persona, he chooses to articulate it through stereotypical Hollywood vocal qualities. Add this to Mason's performance of "So Mexicans Are Taking Jobs from Americans" by Jimmy Santiago Baca, in which Mason chooses to perform the Mexican speaker in a thick Mexican accent. What is so intriguing about Mason's performance is that he, like Kenneth, chooses to add an accent to a piece that has no textual indication that the speaker would sound like that. Unlike Mora, who worked from a text that features dialect, Mason and Kenneth build their vocals from their own perceptions of how these racial groups sound. Thus, the only source of Mason's thick Mexican accent is his own misunderstanding of Mexican culture. Certainly, one could make the argument that the vocals help the audience connect the culture to the piece. But, more intriguing to me is what these accents do. In both these pieces we have white-appearing performers constructing stereotypical representations of cultural others, accentuating the accent based on white Western notions of what Mexicans and Native Americans sound like. These portrayals paint the cultures into neat boxes that too easily allow whiteness to stand as the linguistic cultural norm—one adds culture via dialect. Through the use of the vocals, these white-appearing students construct the other as easily recognizably nonwhite. Whiteness gets normed and rendered the measure by which the Indian and Mexican are presented as vocally different.

In a similar fashion, stereotypical constructs are made about various factions of whiteness in order to distance the white performers from the implications of whiteness. Much like Jerry's use of KKK discourse as a way to other himself from whiteness, Jacob, a white-identified man, refers to another white man as "poor white trash." In this autobiographical narrative, Jacob accounts for this other man's racism through the citation of class and race, rendering himself as the normed and pure antiracist white who can critique others. While much has been done to recover "white trash" (Wray and Newtiz), the use of this stereotype aims to separate the performer from the individual in his narrative. The use of this stereotypical image not only creates a "not-me," but also defines who this other man is: poor, dirty, uneducated, and racist.

Jerry's and Jacob's performances are similar to a final group performance on "white sorority girls." As the performance begins, the three women who make up this group run into the audience and begin passing out flyers urging folks to rush their sorority. The group consists of Sydney, an African American,

Brittany, a white woman, and Mora, an Indian woman, who are nicely dressed and smile broadly as they pass out the printed half sheets of paper. They then run back into the performance space and begin discussing the prospect of joining this sorority. They discuss the benefits of the social group but also note that joining means that they will forever be labeled sorority girls. They disperse to the sides, pause, and return to the center of the room as Brittany squeals "*Oh ... my ... God!*" Each word is punched, articulated with a nod of her head: "You are so in!" The performance continues by showing different aspects of sorority life, featuring several drinking episodes, "frat parties," and fights over each other's boyfriends. The vocals continue to be highly articulated and overly dramatic, as Mora looks at Brittany: "Katie, I mean, *for real?*" This is highlighted by Sydney's mock phone call to her mother in which she explains her desire to join the sorority, overpronouncing each phrase: "Mom! I'm not interested in Rap and all that Boo-Tang! If you had sent me to Highland Heights, then maybe I could relate to my own race!" The performance ends with all three members getting mad at each other, vowing to never be friends again. Sydney ends the piece by saying: "These are actual events. We did an ethnography.[3] It is not meant to make fun. It is political. As one of the participants said, it's just like high school, only no parents." Sydney smiles and the three members sit down as the applause begins.

What is unique in this performance is the fact that it was designed to reflect whiteness as a cultural group. While many final group performances dealt explicitly with racial issues, this was the only one that directly commented on whiteness. However, it is significant that this group examined white sorority girls as a specialized group or subculture within whiteness, focusing on both particular enactments of whiteness as well as the participation by cultural others in these groups. While I wanted to give this group credit for analyzing whiteness, I got more disturbed by the performance as it continued. Rather than critiquing whiteness and cultural power, this performance reinscribed whiteness by creating a representation of it that functioned only at the extremes. The marking of whiteness within the context of white sorority girls, a specialized social grouping often othered in mainstream discourse, and the highly dramatized nature of their talk coupled with the general mocking nature of their performance served to otherize this group just as much as Jerry's southern accent marginalized the KKK member. Thus, what got normalized was the dominant white ideology that was never exposed. Except for Sydney's phone call with her mother, whiteness in general, never got commented upon. This is especially true in that Brittany was named Katie, and was the only actor who is ever named in the entire performance. By naming Brittany "Katie," the performance immediately separated Brittany (and her apparent whiteness) from the whiteness they were critiquing. This extreme othering of white sororities, as well as the authenticity claim Sydney made at the end, serves to marginalize this as a performance of extremism, which in turn serves to relieve mainstream discourse from critique (Daniels). It is precisely these qualities that undermine the possibility that this was a subversive performance of whiteness. By relying on stereotypical reproductions, whiteness, writ large, escapes critique and thus remains invisible as the unmarked cultural center.

In the last several examples, the performers each constructed very particular performances of whiteness through which stereotyping worked to separate the actors from the personae described. This ultimately constructed the performers' own whiteness as nonracist (or at least nonproblematic), while still allowing them to secure the privileged position of whiteness. Whiteness was affirmed and thus unchallenged in their own talk, ultimately reifying the very system that hides, protects, and guarantees white privilege.

While these stereotypical performances of whiteness were present, there were also stereotypes constructed for blackness, such as Janice's performance alluded to in the introduction of this chapter. Janice, a young white-identified woman with long brown hair partially covering one side of her face, sits under soft lighting as she tells the class a narrative based on a "terrifying experience" of being held at gunpoint while working in a video store. She speaks in hushed and somber tones, her chin resting on her knees as she sits in a fetal position on the black plastic chair. The "true story" holds the class's attention; the audience members each sit on the edge of their seats, literally leaning forward toward her. She describes the man who robbed her and notes his black skin, remarking that she was "looking in the face of a mugger." Her narrative concludes with a confession that she now fears this man will get out of prison and search her out. This narrative fascinated me as an audience member, especially as I reflected on how the image of the black man was used to distance Janice from the "mugger." I was first drawn to the way the whiteness of Janice's body, drawn up tight and exposed under the soft lights, was juxtaposed against the narrative of the violent black mugger. While her intent was to share a personal experience, it also served to solidify the stereotypical notion of black men as predators of white women. The availability of this stereotype and the ease with which it was offered demonstrates the power of this particular historical and cultural narrative. The violent black man was served up as an easy source of reference for explicating the fear she had felt at that moment. This stereotype then helped to generate sympathy for her situation. Drawing again on Butler, the summons of the stereotype is an interpellation; Janice's offer of the story and our accompanying acceptance constitutes multiple subjectivities in that moment. She is constituted as victim, the audience is constructed as sympathetic, and the black man is again constructed as always already criminal (Butler, *Excitable*). The moment the audience members either confirm the discourse through silence or physically comfort her at the end of her performance, we take up that discourse and reiterate the stereotypes it offers.

What ultimately gets constructed is a binary between the violent black man and the vulnerable white woman. This binary protects whiteness's social and cultural power in two significant ways. First, whiteness and blackness are clearly separated in this construction. As Janice connects blackness and violence, she disavows herself and her whiteness from that construct. The mugger's blackness, an integral aspect of the narrative, and her whiteness are seen as at odds, in that violence and blackness become inexorably tied together. Janice feeds the stereotype of the violent Black male, thus constituting blackness as more savage, dangerous, and threatening. However, the easy reliance on this stereotype does more than just conflate blackness and savagery, for it also constructs female whiteness as fragile civility that needs protecting. Whiteness's privileged position in this social picture is affirmed, even as Janice acknowledges the problematic nature of her feelings. These citations of racial identity have lasting effects regardless of Janice's intention—they perpetuate racism through a continued naming. As Butler so convincingly argues, "Racist speech works through the invocation of convention; it circulates, and though it requires the subject for its speaking, it neither begins nor ends with the subject who speaks or with the specific name that is used" (*Excitable* 34). By citing the discursive construction of the black criminal, Janice remakes that identity before our very eyes, not necessarily out of desire but through the pervasive power of convention.

Janice was not the only performer to rely on easy stereotypes to affect a construction of cultural others. One could easily reexamine Andrew's performance of "Red Anger," in which he flipped the table as an expression of rage. In this performance, Andrew enlisted a popular vision of blind rage, relying upon whiteness's misunderstanding of cultural anger. In systemic whiteness, white subjects see anger only through the lens of the culture of niceness (McIntyre). This is to say, whiteness expects calm, rational discussion when in conflict, often seeing the expression of passion, excitement, or anger by other cultures as enactments of violence. The flipping of the table as a response or demonstration of Native American anger is a reiteration or reproduction of a cultural stereotype. That the anger has to be expressed through an overt act of violence that destroys material property only reinforces common associations that anger built from racism is a threat to the bodies of whites.

Add to Andrew's performance of rage Joel (bh)'s[4] performance of "Sure You Can Ask Me a Personal Question" by Diane Burns, in which a Native American speaker deals with the multitude of inappropriate questions thrown at her. Joel (bh), a white-identified man with a close crew cut crisply styled with hair gel, begins by walking into the light, his white shirt, black pants, and yellow tie firmly pressed and neatly maintained. He smiles and rubs his hands together, working up the energy to get the performance under way: "The title of my performance is 'Why did I get drunk last night and go to my 8:00 A.M. class!,'" The class laughs as he shakes his head: "Just kidding." The connection of excessive drinking and Native American identity most likely was not intended, but that it was there and so casually offered without critique only serves to reinforce the stereotype of the "drunken Indian." In that one verbal stroke, Joel (bh) promoted and sustained whiteness through the juxtaposition of drinking and Native American identity. Both Andrew and Joel (bh) inadvertently reinscribed stereotypical notions of cultural others, and in their doing so, whiteness was affirmed. Even if the table flip and the drinking comment were not intended to denigrate Native Americans, the associations were nonetheless present and damaging as another reiteration of these stereotypical myths.

While these examples demonstrate the power and utility of stereotypes as performance choices for these students, there were performances that worked to upset the very stereotypes built and reified above. For example, Chu, an Asian man, constructs a performance based in Arab culture, trying to explore the ease with which negative messages of Arab people have been created and maintained through the media. With a towel around his head and sporting a fake machine gun, Chu reaches into his bag and produces a can of cola. With a toss, he announces that it is petrol. Then, he produces another, tosses it into the crowd, and announces that it is a bomb. This is repeated several times, covering several stereotypes of Arab people and noting that these stereotypes are as easy to produce as the colas from his bag. Chu radically co-opts typical stereotypes of Arabs, allowing this cultural group to be examined through the very stereotypes that so often define them. Thus, the towel and fake machine gun, when placed in concert with the deconstruction of additional stereotypes, undermine the very underlying assumption upon which these flawed visions of Arabs are built. This subversive performance did work to interrupt the performativity of whiteness, yet the vast reliance on such negative stereotypes undermined the potential reconstruction that took place in performances like Chu's.

The use of stereotypes was one of the most common ways whiteness got reiterated in these classrooms. This is significant for several reasons. First, the availability of these messages in society and the ease with which one can call upon them details the centrality of whiteness and the concomitant displacing of others. In other words, the fact that each of these stereotypes serves to protect some illusion of white purity demonstrates the security of the cultural center. Second, returning to Butler's notion of disavowal, whiteness grows more powerful through its ability to otherize (*Bodies*). As exercised through these students, the more whiteness displaces other people into marginal categories, the more whiteness becomes the normative identity. It is through the disavowal of these stereotypical others that whiteness gains its status as the center, the dominant, the pure.

Constructing Victimhood:
"I'll admit he scared me, on those long hot August nights.
He probably went through this very town."

The rhetoric of victimhood powerfully constructs an identity difficult to question or critique. The victim is someone you feel sorry for, the one you comfort. To construct the self as victim does very little to allow for dialogue or critical discussion; rather, it shuts down conversation and threatens to render investigation an interpersonal affront. When Janice constructed the image of the black mugger, the face of the man who held her at gunpoint in that video store, I found it very hard to open up her experience for critique. To note the ways she reproduced whiteness in that moment feels like a denial of her experience, a focus that renders her all the more victimized. Yet, the victim construction needs to be studied precisely because of the powerful force behind it. The fact that it eludes critique demands attention, because often the appeal to victimhood serves to mask the construction of privilege that underlies the ability to be victimized in the first place. It is Janice's privilege of whiteness that makes her sympathetic even as she relies on the social script that groups and generalizes all black men into terrifying predators. Janice's performance symbolically constructs every black man as having the potential for violence, violence on her white idealized body. Such a generalization is certainly not Janice's act alone; rather it is to say that because such a script is always already present for white folks to grab onto means that such constructions need to be critically interrogated.

While instances of constructing victimhood are more rare in these classes, the powerful messages embedded within them make this trend significant and deserving of special attention. These performances often take place as side notes, as ways of noting the factors that have contributed to the development of who the performers are. For instance, in his performance, Douglas, a young white-identified man, notes that racism "starts in the home." Here, he justifies racism by claiming that he is an unfortunate result of the pressures created by his home environment. During a moment of autobiographical narrative, Carla notes in her joint performance with Andrew that she lived with her father after the divorce of her parents: "I was raised with his values. I didn't accept them, but they were ingrained into me." In both their performances, Carla and Douglas seek to justify why they have or had particular kinds of values. However, these justifications do more than simply describe the historical creation of their own racism; they also construct themselves as victims, a construction beyond their own agency to change. If racism was "ingrained" in them, then how can they be expected to not be racist—they too are a product of a bad system and thus are not responsible for their own actions. The construction of white victims as products of racist parents simultaneously does two things: First, white victims align themselves with those they oppress—they are as much under the machinery of racism as are people of color and are therefore unable to escape. Second, white victims are constructed as static—figures unable to change because their social role is already formed. That is, they grew up in racist families and are unable to completely throw off that influence. Both of these characteristics function as white talk, removing themselves from the problem of racism (McIntyre). The citation of the racist family is a performative—a reiteration of whiteness that places the white subject outside of the active construction of racism.

In a similar vein, Scott also worked to performatively construct himself as a victim. He begins his intertextual performance with "In the Inner City" by Lucille Clifton: "In the inner-city/or/like we call it/home." Here, Scott pauses, lifting the class anthology, which features literature from America's marginalized cultural voices, and tosses the book to the floor. "I hate this book. It doesn't reflect me at all. It doesn't! I am in agriculture. There is nothing about me in this book." From here, Scott begins to describe life on the farm, incorporating the agricultural creed as a mantra for life. He ends by detailing a moment of saving a calf from dying, noting that "this story is something you can't get out of this book, but that's me. That's my home." Clearly, much is happening in this performance that deserves comment, but what I find most intriguing is the way Scott constitutes himself as a victim of the textbook and its strategic mission to represent that which is so often left absent. The absence of folks like him bothers him, and thus he dismisses the text as incomplete; yet, the irony is that whiteness is already present in this book. In almost every selection that features racism, whiteness is the named or unnamed mechanism or force that contributes to the speaker's inequality. Many times, whiteness is constructed as a force of imperialism, as the force of colonialism, or even directly as the race of the person inflicting harm on others. Scott's resistance not only comments on the absence of white voices from the perspective of white people, but also represents the privilege of whiteness to not see the implications for white subjects in essays and poems about racial inequality. Thus, Scott's construction of himself as absent in these conversations about cultural displacement and social disparities serves to construct himself as the silenced one. In a book about making space for voices that have traditionally been denied, Scott marks whiteness as the silenced victim. This remakes whiteness's normalization, for only that which is always already normed can feel the sudden absence left by the exclusion of whiteness as the dominant perspective. By asserting his own experience at the expense of the cultural others in the text, he reconstitutes whiteness back at the center of the course, the return of whiteness's master narrative.

While blaming family members and pointing out the absence of whiteness in the class performances create two powerful versions of victimhood, there were other performances that actively worked to make whiteness an identity of victimhood. Consider this performance from a group of six students, on serial killers. In this performance, each of the performers appears to be white, though Julian is identified as an international student from Bulgaria. They establish the performance context as a seminar on serial killers, in which each of the members is special agent, except Julian, who is a confessed killer. Julian, the only one marked culturally as different, is physically separated from the others, illuminated by different lights on the other side of the room. After a brief opening statement about how these killers are almost always young white males, each of the speakers rises and gives a brief description of a different serial killer. Each narrative covers the statistics, noting how many people the killer killed and when he was arrested. Nate is one of the last to stand. His performance, however, is more engaged, more direct. He begins, "The Railroad Killer—Angel Resendiz. He doesn't fit the typical profile." Over and over, Resendiz's name is mentioned as Nate peers over his audience. "I'll admit he scared me, on those long hot August nights. He probably went through this very town. He was a serial killer at heart. He killed your grandparents. He raped your wife. He killed and raped your kids. And we couldn't catch him. Be grateful he turned himself in." As he speaks, he leans over the lectern, pointing to individuals each time he notes that a person got killed. When he is done, he slowly turns and sits back down. When the next person mounts the lectern, the statistics resume.

This performance was one of the most fascinating of all the performances I witnessed during my stay in "Performing Cultures." The dry presentation of all those white killers, all the terrible murders that I remember hearing about on television, were presented in almost monotones. The speakers were very distant, very unengaged, until the final speaker began. Nate's narrative addressed the only nonwhite serial killer in the whole performance. Suddenly, the dry delivery became animated; and further, it became personal. These are not just murders, they are murders in *your* family—they are *your* kids. The fact that these details are offered only for the Latino figure makes him the only killer enfleshed for us. Resendiz is a real threat to *this* room, to *this* class, to *our* own bodies. One might explain away Nate's choice by noting that it was the most recent case or that it was of a killer who could have literally been in this Midwestern town, but the personal nature of this description to a room of mostly white students serves to make this raced man a threat to us. Importantly, Resendiz's threat to this room and his nonwhite status cannot be separated, for they are performatively linked. This renders the serial killers coded in whiteness as more neutral, only statistics far removed from the immediacy of this classroom embodied in this Latino killer. Whiteness is constituted as the object of that fear—it is our (white) bodies Nate pointed to, performatively working to make us the victim of this threat.

Finally, I turn to another group performance that strategically constructed whiteness as an identity of victimhood, where it is whiteness that pays the ultimate price for racism. The performance begins in a dance club. Ken, a white-appearing man with red hair, enters and begins gazing admirably at Lakeeshia, a black woman dancing on the other side of the performance space. He walks over and introduces himself. As the performance continues, they begin to date and decide to marry, but as this happens we hear the voices of Ken's family and friends, each of whom decidedly dislikes the fact that he is with her. At one point, Tonya responds to the fact that Lakeeshia's character is pregnant: "Not in this part of the country—a half-breed in these parts?" Suddenly, the lights are turned out and the performers fill the room with hateful racist names, ending with three loud bangs. When the lights are brought back up, Ken lies on the table as if in a coffin, a victim of racism. The final line is offered by the narrator: "Weep not for Ken. He rests in the bosom of Jesus. Will you?"

While the above performance is multifaceted, the death of Ken at the end stands as the most significant aspect of this piece, for it is the white man who dares to date a black woman who dies a victim of the racist machinery. Here, Ken gets constructed as the martyr, as the victim who entered the wilderness of blackness and must pay for his transgression. The whole performance centers on Ken, including the funeral, where it is Ken who gets to address his family and wife from beyond the grave. Ken's life is the subject of this master narrative, a maintenance of whiteness as the narrative center. Even the final utterance by the narrator urging that we not weep for fallen Ken reminds us that this is a tale of what happens when whiteness dares to cross the race line. And while Lakeeshia gets a closing monologue, she and the fate of her unborn child are left unresolved as the lights fade on Ken's body. The performance sets us up to grieve for Ken, to see him as the victim of hatred and racial violence. The foregrounding of this particular construction constitutes whiteness as the ultimate victim of white supremacy, not only separating Ken from the white racists who killed him but also making whiteness fragile, breakable under the weight of racism. Ken is constructed only as victim, only as the subject of racial hatred. This kind of construction makes white people as vulnerable as any other racial group. To be the victim while marked with privilege is the utmost construction of power—not only protected, but unavailable for critique because this production of whiteness has suffered the ultimate price of racism—death.

When students construct images of whiteness as victim, the social power of whiteness grows. When white subjects can be seen as equally under the influence of racism and the social systems of racial punishment, whiteness sheds the responsibility of having to be implicated in the reproduction of racist ideology. Any time whiteness is constituted as victim, the machinery of racial inequality is obscured and rendered absent. The effect of such constructs is a strengthening of whiteness's ability to escape detection, maintaining the purity that comes with the status of the unmarked.

Constructing Whiteness

As I close this analysis, I am brought back to the ways these constructs function to maintain the purity of whiteness. Certainly, none of these performances explicitly denounce the dangers of racial mixing or overtly punish those who cross boundaries. In fact, many of them explicitly advocate just the opposite. However, what is important here is not only the explicit message, but also the implicit messages embedded in the performances. These messages are much more insidious and work much more covertly to construct whiteness as the culturally dominant center. James C. Scott notes that "the public transcript is not the whole story," that for every message there is also a hidden transcript (3). He argues that

> the hidden transcript is produced for a different audience and under different constraints of power than the public transcript. By assessing the discrepancy *between* the hidden transcript and the public transcript we may begin to judge the impact of domination on public discourse. (5, emphasis in original)

This analysis has sought to uncover the hidden transcripts of these performances—to seek out what kinds of messages are present and how they regulate or add to the machinery that regulates the production of whiteness. Thus, the intentions of these performers can be read as a public transcript—a construction that tries to advance, for the most part, a progressive vision of the world. Yet, what also gets constructed are the hidden transcripts—those messages that are so much a part of the ideology of whiteness that they imprint the public transcripts with the taint of privilege, working to retain the pleasure and centrality of their own social dominance. The production of these performances is a production of privilege—a staged production accomplishing whiteness.

Notes

1 It is interesting that Robert passed as white for me the entire semester until this performance. Not only does it demonstrate the instability of race, but also stands as an example of why one should always be wary of declaring another's racial identity without noting that it is one's own reading.
2 See Warren ("Doing") for an extended analysis of Jerry's performance.
3 It is important to note that Schuyler, the instructor for this class, presented a brief account of ethnographic methods, asking students to meet with and learn from members of the cultural

group they are studying. Clearly, these three women have a rather limited understanding of ethnographic methods and the proper way of treating their "participants." In an interview, Sydney noted that she wanted to examine white sororities because she knew of some black women in her residence hall who joined. Sydney then describes one particular woman as an oreo, noting that she "converted": "I try not to laugh. Like, she don't even know how to do her own hair. When the weave is out, it's a mess!" (6 December 1999). Sydney and the women in the group clearly drew on humor and knew they were not presenting a fair account of sorority life.

4 The "bh" in Joel (bh) is to designate Joel's blond hair. There were two Joels that semester and I have intentionally maintained the style of my notation of their names here because these two figures play a prominent part of chapter 5. The other Joel has darker hair, thus is signaled by "Joel (dh)."

Chapter Four

Mundane Accomplishments of Whiteness

Curtis walked in and, again, sat by the door. I've noticed that he keeps sitting there, always the same, always by himself, always in the corner by the door. Kind of tucked into the meeting of the two walls. Kind of hidden. He wears the same forest green ball cap, pulled low over his eyes. He doesn't talk. Even when the class splits into groups, he stays quiet, often needing to be inserted into a group by Renee. I've been watching him, wondering how this performance of self—this everyday, mundane, not marked as special, no-big-deal kind of performance—tells me about race. How might this performance by Curtis, the only African American male in the room, inform me about how race gets produced in the context of everyday classroom practice?

As I begin to write again in my notebook that Curtis sat by himself in the corner by the door, I begin to think about how I am positioning him. I am writing him into a corner in more ways than one. Not only does my (white) ethnographic gaze continue to mark those choices, but I realize that in my (white) obsession with Curtis, I have been reading every choice he makes as racial, all the while ignoring the larger context in which he sits. His decisions I read as racial, while mine and the other white folks in the room somehow escape that same marking, that same racialization. I have continued to write him as different, as other, as he who sits in the corner by the door, while the others go by without comment, without location. It is in that writing that I race him and race myself through negation, through absence, through the maintenance of erasure.

It is here that I realize that my task is more complicated than I originally thought. How do I look at these bodies in new ways? How do I work to see the mundane in new ways? How do I find the ruptures that I know must be there—there in the skip of the record, there in the glitch on the film, there in the gap of the machinery? I know they are there, but I have to find a way to make them visible to myself and others.

As Trinh T. Minh-ha said, "despite our desperate, eternal attempt to separate, contain and mend, categories always leak" (27). Never have I appreciated this reminder more than in my recent attempts to sift through the pages of interview transcripts and fieldnotes to find patterns in how whiteness gets accomplished in the everyday functioning of the "Performing Cultures" classrooms I witnessed. I foolishly assumed that this chapter would follow the lead of the last, patterns arising out of the performances, falling (more or less) into heuristic categories. Yet, I struggled. I discovered that while I could see whiteness manifest on multiple occasions, the instances I had found eluded easy grouping, often blurring, making any scheme uselessly ambiguous—too general or too specific to be productive.

With trouble in my heart, I turned to two colleagues who helped me sort out the problem. In my effort to find categories, I forgot that the central characteristic of whiteness is to continually surface in ways that elide detection. That is, the everyday manifestation of whiteness strategically works to erase its own tracks, to be the blank sheet of paper that holds the image, to be that which we fail to notice. In the everyday maintenance of whiteness as normative, I, as a white man, am meant not to see. The impossibility of making sense of these instances is precisely how whiteness gains its strength as the dominant cultural ideal.

The reminder of whiteness's absence allowed me to return to the staged performances analyzed in chapter 3 and revisit my categories and how they became apparent to me. My experience tells me staged performance heightens the everyday, causing things that might go unnoticed to be made present. Thus, gestures are often enhanced for effect and words are chosen to more carefully carry one's rhetorical message. The staged performances made more visible the production of whiteness, allowing for permeable, yet individually significant, patterns in the construction of whiteness and the maintenance of racial/cultural purity. It was the power of performance that allowed for the gaps in the machinery to become apparent. And while the heightened nature of performance made the constructedness of cultural privilege more visible, the everyday, routinized actions work to do the opposite. These performances are obscured, hidden, and less apparent to the white eyes of this ethnographer. With the heightened articulation of staged performance absent, I lost the clarity with which I was hoping to see the ways whiteness is present in the everydayness of the classroom.

The heuristic nature of staged performance as a way of seeing the production of whiteness, however, not only points to the value of uncovering how students construct messages about race, but also provides an analytic frame for the examination of mundane occurrences of racial maintenance. If the heightened nature of staged performances allows one to see how students make sense of (and reproduce) whiteness, then how might that same typology of performances serve as a way of seeing the everyday workings of whiteness? Thus, I have chosen to replicate the structure of chapter 3 here as a way of seeing how students engaged in the same constructions in slightly different ways. While there are certainly other ways of organizing these instances, I argue that it is productive to examine them within the same frame established by the staged performances, examining the ways similar ends are constructed in differing contexts and with different circumstances.

The categories then serve as a way of seeing more diffuse and more complex instances of whiteness, yet nicely make space for critical interrogation of how whiteness gets maintained in/through interaction. I begin here with constructions of sameness, in which students erased difference in order to secure privilege. Then, I examine how contradictions were constructed in which one message got undermined through hidden or underlying logics. Next, I look at moments in which students relied on or reinforced stereotypes, constructing white normativity through appeals to overly simplistic generalizations. Finally, I ask how constructions of victimhood worked to assert whiteness as oppressed while eliding the very privilege it enjoys.

The instances I examine here arose either through in-class interaction or through individual interviews. While the context certainly affects these performances, I contend that both function as mundane reiterations of whiteness. That is, they derive from educational interactions (teacher-student or ethnographer-student) and allow for students to actively think through their own relationship to issues of culture, power, and privilege, as well as the location of self within that conversation.

Constructing Sameness:
"As long as you keep calling it a race, no one will win."

In the performance rounds, students often professed color blindness, claiming sameness while ignoring difference. This logic played out across several performances, demonstrating the way these acts stem from an illusion of equality while simultaneously reinscribing oppression by blaming those who fail to measure up due to individual faults (Dyer, *White*; Frankenberg; Ryan). This logic is more insidious in mundane performances, rarely surfacing in obvious and distinct ways. Regardless, however, of how this strategic move arose, it did so in ways that secured white privilege, maintaining inequality. The most explicit example of the construction of sameness took place in an in-depth interview with Ryan, a self-identified white woman. In this instance, Ryan constructs whiteness in response to a staged performance from the class: "Carla grew up with a father that was extremely racist. And yet, she came out a well-rounded person with, you know, the ability to see people as being equal regardless of color and look inside, which is what everyone should do." Picking up the common trend in many of the performances in class, Ryan advocates color blindness, suggesting that Carla is to be commended for looking past color. Note also the way the father gets constructed. While surely this characterization of the father as "extremely racist" is made possible by Carla's performance, Ryan reiterates that marking, casting the father as the measure by which both Ryan and Carla establish their enlightenment. Both citations (color blindness and the otherizing of the father) serve to mark the equality among races, demonstrating how whiteness gets performatively constituted through the logic of sameness.

While Ryan directly advocated color blindness, Ellen, a self-identified white woman, erases racial difference in a slightly different way:

jtw: How would you … when you hear the word "race," what does that kind of spark in your mind?

Ellen: Just the term applied to it. I, some kind of quote is like, "As long as you keep calling it a race, no one will win …" or something like that. Have you heard that?

jtw: No.

Ellen: "If you keep calling it a race," something … So like the whole multimeaning of that word. What do I think of when I think of race? Just categories I guess. The category you fall into. If you find that quote, that would be neat. [laughs] Not sure where I first saw it.

This brief exchange in our interview demonstrates a fairly obvious manifestation of color blindness. Ellen relies on a rhetoric of sameness twice in the exchange above. First, she calls upon a "quote" that connects racial identity to a competitive contest without examining the ways racial power begins with unequal conditions. In this way, Ellen critiques race as a meaningful distinction. To name difference means to place people in competition. It is an underlying belief in cultural sameness that allows Ellen to advocate that quotation. Second, and more important, Ellen notes that race is "just categories." It is as if to say that race is simply a box you check on a form, denying the material and discursive violence that takes place along the lines of racial difference. Given her inattention to race as a significant construction, Ellen relies on an imagined equality that is made possible only by her own white privilege (Nakayama and Krizek).

Just as the erasure of difference promotes sameness, so can the appeal to the other, especially if a group of people get marked as other in order to reify normalcy. Consider Renee's spring 1999 class in which she offered a conversation about cultural norms and cultural others. When she asked the class to define the "cultural other," her students began to shout out possibilities: "Not you!" "Out of the expected norm." "Someone you have not encountered." "Behavior distinct from one's own." Immediately, students began to offer individualist notions of *norm* and *other*, seemingly locating difference and sameness within one's own perspective or life experience. Renee continued the conversation the next day, when the appeal to the individual became even more explicit. Marsha begins: "The other are those people who are outside the norm—the extreme." The class continues to describe the characteristics of the other as farther and farther to the margins of society, arguing that people each have "their own norm." Renee, standing at the chalkboard with her hands on her hips, tries to coax them back by asking: "If there is no norm, then why civil rights? Why Matthew Shepherd? I believe there is a standard." Saul nods and raises his hand. After Renee calls on him, Saul states: "Like Jeffrey Dahmer. He totally was not the norm." Renee shakes her head: "You are all interested in extremes here. Take my dad, he's homophobic. Is that normal?" Josh responds: "We all do stuff that's not normal." Again the conversation builds as Renee is overpowered by the students arguing for individual notions of normativity.

Renee, appearing annoyed that the students won't respond as she desires, attempts to gain their attention, raising her hand for silence. As the room quiets, Linda notes: "I lived in Texas, they're totally not normal—very self-centered! Take someone from the Midwest and put them in Europe and they will say they are from America. Put a Texan there, they will say 'I'm from Texas.'" Dallis nods: "I lived in New York. They are not normal either." Renee finally stops class and asks, "Do you hear what you are saying? You know there is a norm. Now think about this Texas and New York thing and apply it to issues of sexuality and race. Is it the same?" The class mumbles but does not grant Renee her point. Almost immediately, Karen notes, "We are all Americans. If you live in America, you are an American."

The class moves directly to extremes, calling upon the logics of individualism, normalcy, and radical otherness, each building toward a performative of sameness. The class does this by beginning with radical individualism, arguing that difference lies in the phenomenological self's relation to others; that is, whether one is normal or not is an individual's determination. Thus, the students constitute the self as asocial, an individually coherent subject existing outside of social norms and social sanctions. Many scholars note the dangers of radical individualism, arguing that such a rhetoric secures the power of the white center (Montag; Scheurich; Treinen and Warren). In particular, Chambers argues that

> whiteness itself is thus atomized into invisibility through the individualization of white subjects. Whereas nonwhites are perceived first and foremost as a function of their group belongingness, that is, as black or Latino or Asian (and then as individuals), whites are perceived first as individual people (and only secondarily, if at all, as whites). (192)

Individualism directly appeals to a rhetoric of whiteness, for only white subjects, socially (and individually) conceived of as normal, can position themselves outside the forces of racial politics. The appeal to such radical individualism is a performative of whiteness—it reifies the notion that we "should be" individuals, all while denying the impact of racism (and other forms of social/political oppression), which makes possible whiteness's invisibility. However, the students do more than simply appeal to individualism. They also move strategically to extremes, calling on Jeffrey Dahmer and "self-centered" Texans as easy exemplars of otherness. Here, certain kinds of difference are judged acceptable to cite as other, allowing the students to occupy less volatile forms of normalcy. It is permissible to argue that mass murderers and specific people from states in the Union are dysfunctional—that these people fall outside the norm; yet, they fail to acknowledge the larger social or political implications of what such a citation means. For it is precisely the appeal to such extremes that allows the semblance of an inclusive normativity to be formed. In other words, through the process of exclusion they engage in, the class is really all the same across color, gender, class, and sexual lines. It functions as a circular contradiction within their own logic—difference or otherness is individual even as we create and sustain a color-blind sameness through the socially marked otherness of the extremes. The circle is completed when Karen argues that we are "all American," falling back on the illusion of sameness secured by the presumption and comfort of white privilege. The whole conversation reiterates whiteness: Whiteness is constituted as normal, difference is rendered invisible, and individualism (and the baggage of meritocracy and individual achievement) is sustained.

The appeal to individualism and the citation of extremes is also present in the interviews. Ryan, a white-identified woman, draws significant comparisons to herself and those marked culturally as other:

> Ryan: Uhm, another example where nobody, you didn't see any stereotypical per-
> formance was when, that sort of dealt with a lot of racial issues, was when Carla
> and Andrew's performance about would he have married her …
> jtw: Oh, right.
> Ryan: Or fallen in love with her if she'd been black. […] I've dealt with that in high
> school where the groups of friends I started out with my sophomore year
> would be classified as sort of freakish, you know? Like, they wore, we were all
> drama people, and were all, they all dressed funky, we had funky hair, the funky
> wardrobes.

Ryan, in this moment, effectively equates being black to participating in the drama club or to wearing a different kind of clothing. The use of "funky" as a descriptor is significant, for often "funky" is used as a derogatory descriptor of blackness—even as the use of language here (funky = drama folks) equates racial politics to school personae. And while the connection of racial difference to her own life experience can help to illuminate her own understanding of racism and systems of domination, she never goes back and reflects on how this minor example (being a drama freak) serves to inform her about racism. When she finishes her drama people story, she is unable to make a serious connection:

> Ryan: I don't know, I think I just got off the subject.
> jtw: No, no I think that's interesting. Especially since in, whereas yours was a mark-
> ing that is done by clothing, that's a lot easier to change and shape than the
> marking of skin color, right?
> Ryan: Unless you're Michael Jackson!
> jtw: Unless you're Michael Jackson …
> Ryan: Ching! [laughs]

As I attempted to draw the conversation back to race, Ryan immediately turned the issue into a joke, loudly saying "Ching," her fist clenched and moved downward as if to demonstrate a cash drawer. Thus, the attempt to make a meaningful connection from her life to the conversation about race ends with Ryan's style differences equally ranked with racial difference. The Michael Jackson citation is an additional move toward extremism, locating difference in the spectacular racial complexity of Jackson. This reference not only resecures the stability of her comparison and performatively reestablishes her privilege to equate those elements of difference, but effectively erases the significance of race as a marker at all. Thus, whiteness and color are rendered the same.

While the previous examples each relied on contexts in which race was addressed explicitly, there were times when whiteness was being reconstituted without participants directly talking about it. Consider this moment from Emmitt's interview in which he begins by discussing Joel (bh) as a player and then shifts to a conversation about rebellious behavior (2 May 2000):

> Em: I think [being a player]'s a characteristic of his culture.
>
> jtw: Would you identify that with any particular kind of group that he might belong to, or would you say...
>
> Em: I think that's just him. Like, his personality.
>
> jtw: Do you think culture is individual then? Is it Joel's culture or does it tie in with, so any of these characteristics tie in with a larger group?
>
> Em: Uh ... I think, well, it's individual if you want it to be. Like I said, if you're a rebel, then you're going to make your own culture. A case in point: Dennis Rodman. Marilyn Manson. Okay? How many people have a culture that are like those? But, then if you're a person like me who was born into a small town, has heritage in the south, I didn't really make my own culture, I learned it. And I didn't rebel. So I decided to keep that culture. So I think it can be learned and if you learn it and you don't like it, you can make one of your own. You know what I mean? And I just adopted that culture I was born. [...] You know Marilyn Manson rebelled. [laughs]

While Emmitt is not explicitly discussing race, he does talk about culture here in some meaningful ways. He begins by defining culture in the broadest sense, avoiding any reference to gender, race, or class. When he does this, he effectively renders culture so broad and ambiguous that culture is anything one chooses it to be. In fact, Emmitt goes so far as to claim that people can create their own culture, rendering culture as interchangeable as articles of clothing. With such simplicity, culture becomes a meaningless concept that is erased of any specificity or sociality. And since it is defined by choice, individuals are understood to have the power to identify with or negate any element of difference. In this way, culture becomes highly individualized—it is something that one can choose to keep or choose to rebel against. This makes culture solely an element of choice, erasing society's role in the constitution of its subjects.

In these passages, Emmitt is talking about difference, and what he says has implications for how whiteness, as a performative, gets repeated. Every time Emmitt locates movement from the center to margins as choices that one can make (Manson chooses not to conform—to rebel), he locates difference as an enactment of only individual agency. Emmitt reduces difference to a choice, rendering all difference or marginalization an exercise of one's free will—one has the privilege not only of choosing whether one wishes to be different, but one's choice becomes an exercise of individual intent. Thus, Emmitt constructed everyone as beginning from the same general location, and those who fall to the margins do so through exercising choice. Emmitt says, "I decided to keep that culture," confirming his position in the privileged center as a choice or acquisition he can make. To locate difference and power in individual choice is an effective reiteration of whiteness's power and a significant construction of sameness, especially when Emmitt locates Dennis Rodman and Marilyn Manson as exemplars of rebelliousness. The move to Rodman and Manson as examples of those "outside" the norm is interesting for those individuals are celebrities—such constructions of otherness are exactly how Rodman and Manson maintain their celebrity status. Thus, the extreme examples Emmitt draws on are rebels only inasmuch as they need that perceived marginalization to promote and sustain their own professional location in popular culture.

Emmitt was not the only one to construct sameness through direct appeals to individual choice. A particularly interesting variation took place in a class conversation revolving around issues sparked by Dwight Conquergood's model of ethical performance ("Performing") and performer empathy. Joel (dh) responds to those who advocate creating an empathic relationship between performer and text:

> Empathy can be bad. Sometimes, I don't give empathy—these people use this stuff as crutches and I'm not one to help one stay down. I'm in debt up to my eyeballs but I'm just glad to be walking and talking. Get over this and keep going. I can say I do know how you feel. But then I say I did this, I overcame. Now you can, too. I hate weak people. They make me sick.

Ross Chambers' argument that only whiteness enjoys the pleasure of individualism and the subsequent benefits of meritocracy can help to illuminate the way Joel (dh) levies power rhetorically based on his own ingrained individualism, which assumes that others have that privilege as well. Note how Joel (dh) both misuses empathy, rendering it a thing rather than a relationship, while also powerfully constructing individualism by naming people who might inspire empathy as "these people." In that citation, Joel (dh) performatively reconstructs the myth of meritocracy, noting that it is only through individual choice that one "stay[s] down." He continues to insist, "I did this, I overcame. Now you can, too." Joel (dh)'s rhetoric of meritocracy performatively reconstitutes failure as an individual shortcoming that blames the victim both for his position of marginality in the system and for invoking the systemic inequalities as a site of his oppression (Ryan). Consequently, both the positionality and the presumption of cultural critique are framed as individual weaknesses or pathologies unworthy of inciting empathy from those whose "merits" exclude them from oppression.

As I close this discussion of sameness as a rhetorical strategy of whiteness, I would like to turn to my interview with Sydney, an African American student who reflected on a performance from class. In her autobiographical performance of being pulled over and threatened by a racist police officer, Sydney details to the class what it felt like to be a small woman of color in the hands of a large, strong, white man with a gun:

Syd: I feel that story needed to be told.

jtw: What do you mean, that it needed to be told?

Syd: That the fact that it's 1999 and me and my roommate are scared to travel home at night. We'll leave in the morning 'cause at night we get pulled over, that officer could have raped and killed us and no one would have known. I mean, she had her cell phone, but he could have did anything [sic] and we was three females and we didn't. ... Normally, we do carry knifes [sic] and stuff, but we had left them 'cause we was thinking it was broad daylight. But ...

jtw: It's true, 'cause I ... it's true in terms of I don't think that audience ... if I was eighteen, nineteen in that room, I could see myself very much not believing that that kind of thing could actually happen.

Syd: Tight. And a lot of people in that room, they don't ... They're like, you're just black, but you don't understand what it's like. You can go into Dillards or whatever and no one spies on you. No one's going to check your bag. You can go home whenever you want, no one's going to pull you over and give you a fifty-dollar ticket for not wearing your seatbelt. And your boyfriends or whatever come down to visit you and it's not a big thing and people are not scared, you know?

jtw: Scary issues. [...]

Syd: Right. I mean, sometimes I feel ignored, like [sarcastic voice] *oh, well that's so dramatic—that's so bad and oh, well ... I understand!*

jtw: So it's kind of like, well, that's *just* one story.

Syd: I just wanted them to know. That's all. That was my only purpose.

Sydney's narrative of race relations takes a very different perspective on the issue of sameness even while it marks the prevalence of sameness as a classroom theme. She clearly privileges difference when she narrates the experience of surveillance in a Dillard's department store. However, she also powerfully locates the appeal to sameness as an expected and unreflective response from her classmates. She denies sameness, pointing out the illogical nature of the sameness construction while simultaneously acknowledging whiteness's role in systems of racism and privilege. When she sarcastically characterizes the other students' reaction as: "That's so dramatic—that's so bad," she critiques the very assumptions that underlie white privilege. She seems to know that this citation of racial difference in a space where sameness is continually being constructed won't effect change, yet still feels it is her job to offer this competing narrative that foregrounds social difference along racial lines. Sydney's commentary deconstructs the myths of individualism and meritocracy, demanding that the erasure of racial difference and the illusion of sameness needs to be questioned. In effect, Sydney completely subverts the construction of sameness promoted in this classroom.

However, Sydney's efforts, when placed in the context of these repeated and strongly defended performatives of sameness, are in many ways co-opted. These kinds of comments can be used to build up the very construction of sameness Sydney is trying to resist, for Sydney is one (individual) voice in a room full of adamant color-blind advocates. The very context of the classroom constitutes her as an individual subject, appropriating her voice to serve the machinery of whiteness that she seems to be struggling to resist. It is the power of whiteness to take resistant messages and use them as fuel for the continuation and maintenance of purity.

The construction of sameness, while not as explicit as sometimes presented in the class's staged performances, effectively works along the same lines by performatively making and remaking cultural privilege. Taken as a whole, these reiterations serve to persistently and continuously reinforce a cultural myth, specifically individualism and meritocracy, which rely on a rhetoric of sameness in order to secure white privilege.

Constructing Contradictions:
"Most mascots are done in full headdress and it is more of an honoring of Indians, not an insult."

In chapter 3, I found several examples of contradictions or moments in which differing messages rubbed against each other in performance in ways that undermined the rhetorical intent claimed by the performer. It was much more difficult to locate contradictions in mundane performances. I suspect the reason for this lies in the nature of whiteness as a system that self-regulates in everyday life. As Butler reminds us, whiteness is a "construction that regularly conceals its genesis"—whiteness is performed in such a naturalized way that the gaps, those moments of contradictory messages, are hard to find (Butler, "Performative" 273). Nevertheless, I did find moments in interviews and class interactions that, when viewed through the lens of contradiction, provide a heuristic way of seeing whiteness in action. In the following examples, I analyze how moments of contradiction reveal how whiteness often relies upon occupying two apparently contradictory stances.

The first example of contradiction stems from my interview with Karen.[1] Karen strongly positions herself against political correctness: "I'm not terribly politically correct. Don't aspire to be." She then proceeds in the interview to reinforce common messages of racism ("we're getting reverse discrimination [...] against white males") and heterosexism ("I don't dare voice my opinions about homosexuality because it would not be politically correct"). Karen often offers explicit statements that secure and reproduce whiteness:

> So I don't know, it will be interesting to see in another twenty years how all this [mocking tone] *multiculturalism* plays out. Is it just the buzzword of the nineties that comes and goes? And my fear is that some people are so radical about it that it almost becomes offensive. I mean, I say I'm not politically correct and I have no intentions of being, because I'm offended by the extremist reaction of political correctness. You know? That offends me.

This segment contains a key internal contradiction that is worth examining. Karen claims to be "offended" by political correctness. The juxtaposition of her own sense of offense and her not being able to freely offend others strikes me as a powerful way of attacking political correctness through the very logic of political correctness. Karen feels herself victimized by political correctness and argues that this inability to speak her own mind silences and marginalizes her. In refusing to be silenced in the name of political correctness, Karen articulates both the position and the pain of marginalization. The logical contradiction here is that only through the privilege of whiteness can one occupy both positions—to be offended at the inability to offend others. This specious claim to marginalization and victimization based on the historical privilege of offending others powerfully reconstitutes whiteness through the use of contradictory stances.

Karen's statement in this segment of the interview is contradicted later in the conversation in ways that also strongly reproduce whiteness's discursive power. While Karen works to deny the impact of dominant culture, she is very vocal about how messages of privilege in regard to beauty standards get reproduced in the media. She argues that "the media defines the values of our country," and "in the media, we see beauty defined pretty much eighty percent, not exclusively, but eighty percent of our beauty as white, thin, good looking, beautiful—come on, *beautiful* people are in!" This creates an interesting contradiction in that Karen consistently reproduces white privilege through her attacks on political correctness, yet she also acknowledges and blames the media for privileging certain kinds of people. That she can recognize and critique the media as the only source for reproducing privilege while participating in the very mechanisms that maintain everyday racist ideologies performatively remakes her whiteness in powerful ways. She gets to dismiss political correctness as extremist while simultaneously taking a critical stance against popular messages of normativity as played out in beauty standards. Whiteness benefits through her attack on equal rights efforts (under the guise of political correctness) while at the same time benefiting from appearing to be critical of discriminatory messages. Karen protects whiteness through these attacks even while constructing whiteness as a position that is both aware of and concerned about how power gets used to privilege and oppress people. It is in these two contradictory positions that whiteness is sustained and removed from critique through an illusion of self-reflexivity.

Karen's criticism of political correctness resurfaces several times in the interview, most strongly in the following:

> And I certainly *resent* an ideology [political correctness] that says you're not looking at what I did—you're picking on me because I'm different ... and we don't do that anymore. [pause] I don't know, I think in some ways people use that to their advantage. And maybe I'm just unhappy about it because I'm not one of those people who can use it to my advantage. I don't know.

In this brief segment, Karen not only distances herself from the struggles of people of color and gays and lesbians (as if her position as a heterosexual, married, white woman is not implicated in those struggles), but actually suggests that there is an advantage to being marginalized. Karen's line of attack is familiar, having long been used by opponents of affirmative action programs and other initiatives that work to equalize opportunity. The problem lies in its internal contradiction: The attempt in these programs and in the logic of political correctness is to equalize what is already inherently unequal. When opponents argue that such initiatives create an advantage, they ignore historically established inequalities such that the advantage they speak of (and condemn) is simply the threat of equality. This attack strategically works to maintain inequality, thus protecting the sanctity of privilege.

Finally, Karen's attack on political correctness and "certain aspects" of the multicultural movement is particularly troubling when juxtaposed with her feelings about obesity:

> Gosh, I don't see anybody saying, you know, let's stop the fat jokes. Somebody makes a fat joke ... I don't know, would people be upset about that? You know? I think that is offensive. I've been on both sides of that. I was anorexic in high school—I was extremely skinny. I've never been obese, but I [pause], I call it putting on my winter fur. And I know how painful it is just to have my husband make little comments, you know, that aren't meant to be hateful, but just are inconsiderate and how hurtful that is to me. That ... I can't imagine how awful it would be to hear those comments on a *regular basis*. Or to have people literally just stop on the street and stare at you.

The great care and sympathy Karen gives to obesity is interesting not only because she seems to grant that there is a social oppression that goes along with carrying weight, but also in her connection of obesity to her own struggles with her size. Suddenly, the immediacy of this issue in her life grants it legitimacy, making weight a genuine reason for concern. The fact that Karen can choose which forms of systemic discrimination actually exist demonstrates how powerful the position of privilege is that Karen occupies. The ability to deny certain kinds of inequalities because they don't negatively impact her locates her at the center of every discourse of oppression, making her the arbitrator of when something is discriminatory and when it is not. This contradiction in her interview not only undermines her desire for everyone to be able to voice their opinions, but it also weakens her attacks on political correctness, for she relies on political correctness even as she attacks it. This construction of contradiction performatively remakes whiteness, for only whiteness can occupy these divergent positions. Looking at Karen's contradictions as performatives of whiteness, it seems clear that by dwelling in the space of competing messages, racial, sexual, and other such norms remain relatively free from critique and the possibility for transformation.

In a very different manifestation of contradiction, Sydney engaged in an interesting example that, while not necessarily remaking white privilege, worked to regulate racial identities, thus securing whiteness as normative. Consider this portion of our interview, in which Sydney discusses the preparation for her group performance on white sororities:

Syd: And I interviewed this black girl, but she didn't, how shall I say, converted to you'all very nicely. She's not the type of black girl I am. She's *really* converted. [laughs]

jtw: What does that mean for you—to say that?

Syd: To be honest, I call her "oreo." And what that means is she's black on the outside, but in her heart she's a white girl. [laughs]

jtw: What kind of things tell you that?

Syd: She ... she [high-pitched voice], "oh my god" and ... and it's not even that her boyfriend's white. Her room is just junky as I don't know what. It's just nasty. I have to interview her and I'm like, and I don't want to bring her to my room 'cause she's nasty so ... but she's uhm ... she's a white girl. ... And she's, uhm, she's very dark. She's dark complexed [sic] and me and my roommate are like, she's the blackest thing in here and she's is so white. She wears the curly weave—and it's like, so funny.

jtw: So there it seems like, there's something in the way in which she moves through the world. And so it's an issue of hair, it's an issue of room, relationships ...

Syd: Right. But I didn't assume, I could just tell by the way she talked that she was an oreo. And I had met her like two years earlier before when I had to take a test at downtown Chicago to NSI [Necessary Skills Institute]—are you familiar with that program?

jtw: Uh huh.

Syd: And I had to take a test and she talked and talked the whole time and I didn't look behind me and I thought it was a white girl and it wasn't and I was like, that's the blackest thing in here and you are so white.

Sydney's talk, as Butler would remind us, functions as a discursive critique of blackness by rendering a charge that the other black girl is not really black ("Performative"). This critique drives to the heart of essentialist race categories, signaling that skin color can be superseded by one's enactment of race. Yet, Sydney's construction of this black woman is significant when juxtaposed to her description of blackness as an essential marker of identity: "Whatever you do in life, you're going to be black. You're going to be the black doctor, the black lawyer, the black criminal, whatever. That's how society looks at you. Whatever I do, you're going to be black." Since Sydney constructs blackness here as an essential characteristic of racial identity, the inconsistency occurs between conceptions of race: Race is performance centered ("she's a white girl") versus race is essential ("you're going to be black"). This contradiction is not inconsequential, for when Sydney makes such contradictions, whiteness, as a performative identity, gets reified as the normative, dominant racial category. When Sydney argues that the other unnamed black girl is "really" white, she marks such a performative move as a betrayal—the "conversion" that this black woman underwent denies blackness in favor of an enactment of whiteness. This critique can seemingly locate blackness as the normative broken by the woman, but such a construction fails when Sydney argues for essential blackness based on skin tone. This desire to keep blackness stable is an effort to maintain racial categories and the distinction and recognition of whiteness as oppressively dominant. Still, the betrayal in this woman's performative enactment of whiteness is a signal that when blackness is broken, whiteness prevails. It is not accidental that this woman's alternative performance is whiteness—it is not accidental that this woman appeals to the culturally dominant racial category. But because Sydney holds on to essential race categories that are tied to skin tone even as she notes this other woman's performative betrayal, it is whiteness that remains normative. Such a construction recenters whiteness, even as Sydney works to decenter it.

In the context of the classroom, students' interactions relied on contradictions in ways that offered variations on the themes of contradiction that emerged in the interviews. In the following example, contradiction occurs when students advocate sameness while simultaneously constructing powerful messages of difference that secure their own cultural power. In a class discussion on culture and the use of ethnic and racial groups as school mascots, Schuyler, the instructor, attempts to problematize the use of racial others in ways that reinstitute oppression. The members of the class involved in the conversation are Amie, Madison, Mark, Connie—all of whom appear to be white—and Sydney.

Schuyler begins a discussion of an assigned reading that asks questions about what culture is and how cultures function and interact. Amie asks the class about the use of Native American images as mascots for school teams,[2] noting that her school had to change its mascot for the Raiders because "it was an Indian." She continues: "Most mascots are done in full headdress and it is more of an honoring of Indians, not an insult."

Connie notes that she once knew someone at the University of Illinois who was the mascot for the Fighting Illini: "He was one hundred percent Irish. He had to be inducted into the tribe to do it." Madison says in agreement, "That's honoring them." Amie raises her hand: "You never hear about the training, you only hear the using parts."

Mark, a young man who begins by noting his Irish descent, remarks, "I don't know about the 'Fighting Irish,' but I once heard someone make a comment in a bar about drinking and the Irish. Someone says to me, 'Are you Irish?' Yeah, it doesn't really bother me, but it's the same principle."

Sydney, the only black woman in the class, immediately follows: "I don't like names like the 'Redskins.' It's like calling them the Houston Honkeys! "Redskins," I have a problem with 'cause it's like name calling." A subtle chuckle ruffles through the classroom after Sydney speaks, but soon the comment is lost in the continuing discussion. Sydney sits back and remains silent for the rest of the class.

Whiteness gets reproduced here through several contradictions. First, defense and protection of Native American mascots sanctions the continual marginalization of Native Americans by exploiting a people's history and culture for a sports team. Further, the class's discourse itself reifies the contradictions that make it possible for these images to exist. By referencing the training and cultural sensitivity of the individual wearing the mascot "costume," the act of cultural appropriation is rendered benign—an "honoring" of the other. The assumption here is that the team is white (or at least the culture that owns and consumes sports is white), thus the use of the ethnic other serves as a cultural counterpoint—the signifying marker of an unmarked invisible center. Whiteness needs the mighty Indian Brave or the Redskin to bring presence in the absence of whiteness. Whiteness gets protected in this class by marking nonwhiteness as something that can be taken up as a borrowed image, a representation of something lacking. The meaningful contradiction here is that while students want to claim that Native American mascots honor rather than insult they rely implicitly on the privilege of normative whiteness and the concomitant marginalization of cultural others in order for the possibility of mascots to work in the first place. That is, without the logic of a cultural center and margins, the Native American would not make sense as a meaningful mascot. Its rhetorical power demands the existence of the very inequality that the students deny.

Additionally, if we consider the comments by Mark, the young man who connects his Irish background to that of Native Americans, we see whiteness getting constructed through a different contradiction. Mark notes his Irish descent but fails to make clear the values he places in that ethnicity. He never offered that label in class before, and further, he was never marked in that way by anyone else in the class. The citation of Irish identity serves as a way to speak with authority about labeling "others," yet fails to recognize the different stakes in those identities. Mary Waters argues that "symbolic ethnicity persists because it meets a need Americans have for community without individual cost and that a potential societal cost of this symbolic ethnicity is in its subtle reinforcement of racism" (qtd. Nakayama and Krizek 302). Thus, Mark's ability to draw on his Irish identity in order to dismiss the damage that mascots constitute renders the "insult" insignificant. After all, if the image of the drunken Irish doesn't "bother" him, then why should Redskins bother Native Americans? It is in the incompatible meeting of Mark's "symbolic ethnicity" and the more culturally relevant ethnicity implicated in the appropriation of Native American heritage that whiteness gains its strength.

It is also worth noting the erasure of Sydney's comment that points out the double standard, indicating that a reverse "honoring" of the Houston Honkeys would never survive as a cultural mascot. As one of two women of color and the only African American in the class, Sydney's comment is offered at great risk. When her point is taken as a joke, enfolded in amused chuckles, she becomes silent, effectively erased. The amusement itself illuminates the absurdity of having a culturally derogatory white mascot. But Sydney's erasure does more than silence her—it produces whiteness as well, for only the white students' comments are taken seriously in the flow of the conversation. The students reconstitute whiteness during this classroom interaction by asserting whiteness's normativity at the expense of Sydney's dissenting voice.

Each of the performative contradictions that emerged in this conversation asserted white privilege and cultural dominance by reiterating whiteness as the dominant identity category, the "pure" cultural center. The contradictions juxtapose the logics of sameness: The race of the mascot doesn't matter, it is not racist, while simultaneously the mascot is not us, not white, thus marking the otherness of the nonwhite category. These contradictions performatively reiterate the centrality of whiteness as dominant.

The contradiction of sameness is also captured in Ellen's interview, where she reflects on her performance of interracial dating:

Ellen: But the second [performance] was, I think, the more meaningful for me to look
         into. I mean, I had *Ebony* magazines and all my sources laid out and my parents
         walked by and my dad said, "what's that!" An interrace magazine. And I just
         kind of let him panic for a moment and then said it was a project and he went

"oh, good!" I mean, he was sincerely worried about why I had this. They come from ...

jtw: It's based in the whole idea of what it means to be in a normal relationship?

Ellen: Yeah. I try to be more open-minded than my parents. [...] I wouldn't call them racists, I mean that's a bit too strong for their condition, but they definitely have something against minorities, African Americans especially. And if they know someone who is dating a black person, they'll be like, "Do you know who she's dating? They had a kid together."

jtw: What is your opinion?

Ellen: It's cool ... interracial relationships. I personally am not attracted to any men that aren't white. I had a few dating experiences like that, but [pause] I think it is perfectly fine.

These series of statements by Ellen are fraught with internal contradictions. On the one hand, Ellen appears to advocate dating outside one's race, and the very choice of interracial dating as the topic of her performance affirms this. Yet in the interview, Ellen pauses after "It's cool" and drops her pitch, suggesting some sort of hesitation to fully embrace the idea. Then, she asserts her own purity by denying that she is attracted to nonwhite men, followed by a reluctant approval of the idea of making such a choice. Further, her claim to have dated someone from another race and her refusal to do it any more cites the authority of experience. Not only do racial categories get reified through the marking and separation of racial groups, but whiteness is further secured by serving as the arbitrator of whether it is permissible to mix. Ultimately, Ellen relies on a lukewarm tolerance of racial unions, while preserving her ability to avoid such relationships. Her contradictions and hesitations negate her overt message of acceptance. Finally, contradiction is exasperated by Ellen's denial that her parents are racist, even while they "definitely have something against minorities." In this utterance, Ellen is able to acknowledge that she is better than her parents even though she protects them from the stain of racist tendencies. When she jokingly "let [her father] panic for a moment," Ellen contradicts the overt message of her performance by claiming "this is just a project" for school. Her joking with her father minimizes the topic and reinstates the sanctity of white-on-white relationships. Ultimately, this message functions to resecure the dominant culture, preserving whiteness as an ideal that she, regardless of her performance, plans to maintain. Whiteness is constructed in the contradiction between what Ellen advocates publicly to the class in performance and what she is willing to share with me in the interview, rendering her whiteness unchecked by the rhetoric of her own performance.

In a final example of contradiction, Ryan spoke in her interview about Tom's performance of Laurence Thomas' "Next Life, I'll Be White," drawing very different conclusions than the text or performance had foregrounded:

> Yeah, next time I come back I'll be a white man. And it was just, it was interesting, it was weird to see a white male playing a black male wanting to be white. I mean, that took a lot of guts to do something like that 'cause, uhm, in a society where everybody is supposedly equal and a lot of people claim that we're not to get up there and do that and say a black man wants to, to take a poem when you're a white male and say that a black male wants to be white. I mean that can get a lot of stuff thrown in your face.[. . .] I don't remember when the poem was written, I remember looking at it and at the time you could understand why the person who wrote it, like, that wanting, 'cause it was back when, a time before the civil rights movement when blacks were not equal to whites, so blacks sort of wished they were in a white man's skin, you know? The poem was written to say this is what's happening to me, I'm slaving, I'm doing all this and I can't be your equal, so when I come back I want to be here. Instead, like if it were written afterwards, I think it would have been different. I think it would have been more like, I'm proud of who I am, you know?

It must be noted that Ryan was present during the performance and postperformance discussion and that she claims to have read the essay in the textbook. Thomas' piece is contemporary; not only does the textbook biography locate his writing in the past two decades, but the text itself describes current struggles of African American men. The claim to be "white in the next life" is a metaphor for the desire for equality—to enjoy the public trust afforded white men in this society. Ryan not only dramatically misreads the author, the essay, the performance, and the postperformance discussion, but then continues to honor that misreading as a risk taken by this white performer. What does the discursive repetition of white privilege, as formulated in this contradiction, construct in that moment? How does whiteness gain power through the inaccurate citation of it as the ideal that this black man desires? At the meeting of misreading and the actual text arises a claim to authority—here is a black man yearning to be equal, yearning to be normal, yearning to be white. By locating that desire in Thomas' piece, Ryan easily recenters whiteness through a performative of white superiority that demonizes blackness as the contaminant that makes equality impossible.

As I close this section, I would turn to a moment in Diana's interview when she reflects rather eloquently on a contradiction that took place in her class during the conversation about cultural norms and cultural others:

> I wouldn't have felt comfortable talking about [my understanding of cultural norms] in class because I understand the sort of environment we're in and what [Renee] was trying to get across. I try not to work against what she's doing with her class ... is that there *is* a norm. There *is* a norm that I think our society works under. And that norm is white, the norm is male, the norm is middle or upper class, the norm is educated.[. . .] Like if someone told me, think of a man. That's the kind of man I'd probably come up with, just instinct. [. . .] You want to think the world has moved past that and we don't feel those things any more. So, that's why I wouldn't have engaged those things—I wouldn't have spoken up.

Diana is clearly reflective about contradictions between how the world operates and the ways the class narrated intercultural dynamics. She acknowledges that there is a race, gender, and class norm and she seems to be beginning to analyze the effects of this norm in her life. More than anyone else I interviewed, Diane had thought the most about issues of privilege and power. This reflection is captured in her deconstruction of Renee's class, in which she locates the cultural strategy of whiteness working in the classroom. She told me frankly that the dominant cultural logic wants to "think the world has moved past that [racism]"; however, Diana herself maintains that there is a norm at work in the classroom. She seems to realize that this moment is contradictory, yet appears to understand the persuasive power of the class's logic. Diana may have let the contradiction protect white privilege in the classroom interaction, but she clearly understood how power was functioning in that moment, deconstructing it outside the classroom by making it a heuristic space for critique.

The staged performances analyzed in chapter 3 demonstrated how contradictory messages in performance worked to secure and maintain whiteness as a pure and protected identity. Here, the mundane performances as critiqued in the interview reflections and classroom fieldnotes do roughly the same thing. They do so, however, in more obscure and insidious ways. The subtle contradictions in these students' conversations about race and culture show how pervasive whiteness is as a cultural reproduction and how difficult it is to facilitate critical reflection on white privilege.

Constructing Stereotypes:
"In some, it's just a head thing."

In chapter 3, I described how students often relied on stereotypes in order to both otherize persons of color and remake whiteness as a privileged identity. I found the everyday reliance on stereotypes just as explicit as the staged citations, a repetition that is different than the previous themes I've addressed. In a particularly clear manifestation of stereotypes, Ken offered the following in a class conversation on performing gender: "I mean, it's like in the Middle East where women must walk behind and go into different doors!" In that off-hand comment, Ken relied on a stereotype of Middle Eastern cultures in order to enable his own whiteness, as well as his own nationality, which is coded with racial overtones, to serve as the mark by which those others fail to measure up vis-à-vis his presumption of gender equality. Regardless of whether the students realized the construction of stereotypes or not, these occurrences worked to reaffirm and reconstitute whiteness as the cultural center.

In many cases, the students noted their use of stereotypes even as they offered stereotypical characterizations of others. For example, Ryan discusses a debate about student government and the number of African Americans in office:

> Ryan: And then, the debate just went on about how blacks were never going to be in positions of power so we have to go this route to get things done. And, like, the whole debate, it was just like here we are supposed to be an equal society and people are still talking about how blacks are suppressed and all this stuff. And in some cases it's true and in some it's not and in some, it's just a head thing. I don't know.
>
> jtw: Can you talk about what that means? What do you mean about sometimes it is...
>
> Ryan: I feel like I'm digging myself into a hole...

As evidenced by her final line, Ryan knows she is using a racial stereotype. Regardless, I find the "blame the victim" language noteworthy, for it demonstrates how powerful the act of naming is (Butler, *Excitable*; McKerrow). The power to name an experience, to call into question another's experience, is to assert one's cultural power through a performative—to name is to discursively constitute. When Ryan argues that "it's just a head thing," she renders the experience of others as solely the product of their own imaginations. Ryan calls upon the myth of meritocracy to critique African Americans, noting that they are "still talking" about their own situation with respect to things that Ryan clearly doesn't believe exist. The citation of her belief trumps anything that was said in the debate she referred to, making her whiteness the ultimate judge of black experience.

Stereotypes surface in another way in my interview with Ellen:

Ellen: You know, if someone of a race that traditionally is known to be an over-achiever—the whole class is an overachiever and [if] they're not for once, you wonder what's wrong with them. Or vice versa. So they got to live up to expectations.

jtw: So it's like the issue of categories again? We're being held to categories—just trying to play your part ...

Ellen: Yeah, and if you don't fit into that category, then something is abnormal about you—not your race, just you. Or sometimes, it is applied to that race. You know? The stereotypical idea that Asians are really good in math. If someone's not, then they're a disgrace to their ... [laughs]

While Ellen is clearly reflective of the fact that the stereotypes she calls upon are indeed generalizations, she never offers a critique of this strategy. Instead, she ends her commentary with a giggle, stopping her from offering a potentially subversive angle on the stereotypical image of Asians as proficient in the hard sciences. This stereotype is just how it is—the "overachiever" just has to "live up to expectations." By failing to speak back to that stereotypical characterization of Asian culture, Ellen reiterates it.

While each of the examples I have discussed rely on naming the other while excluding whiteness and white speakers from the production of those messages, an interesting trend arose in multiple interviews and class moments in which students relied on subtle stereotypes that reproduced whiteness. Consider the following example from class in which the students describe their affective response to a performance by Lakeeshia, an African American student:

Lucy: Do you like this speaker?
Ken: Yes and no.
Tonya: Confident.
Cathy: She *is* confident!
Nate: Intimidating—she felt like that.
Ken: It depends on how you were raised. I was raised not to brag.

While no one raised race as a signifier of Lakeeshia's performance, I find it interesting that the students focused their talk immediately on the confident nature of this speaker, even signaling that she was bragging. What does it mean that the first response to this speaker was that she was inappropriately bragging? How does this critique, built from comments surrounding the paralanguage of her performance, connect Lakeeshia's blackness, her confident tone, and the cultural inappropriateness of bragging? Delpit notes that many white students ignore the content of what students of color say, focusing instead on their vocal qualities. If one juxtaposes the classroom moment centered on Lakeeshia's vocals with several comments from my in-depth interviews, one sees how such a focus is a culturally informed move:

Sport: Different people talk in different ways. I just interpreted it as it means. I don't try to put my own spin on it to understand it, I go on what I've learned from different people like my parents or friends or grandparents.

jtw: Do you see other people doing different stuff with it?

Sport: I see a lot of people, a lot of people have their own ways of performing culture ... like, emotionally or loudly.

jtw: What do you mean loudly?

Sport: They like to show a lot of emotion when performing cultures.

jtw: Do you see people in the classroom performing culture everyday, in their everyday ways in which they interact? Do you see this in the class at all?

Em: Yeah, definitely.

jtw: Can you give me any examples of places or times?

Em: I would have to, I'd use Lakeeshia as a pretty good example.

jtw: Okay.

Em: Like whenever we have class discussion, she's always raising her hand and having something to say. Every discussion.[. . .] And she's always, and whenever she speaks, she always speaks loud and clear and she emphasizes what she wants, what she needs to.

In these segments from Sport's and Emmitt's interviews, we see how this focus on vocal qualities gets further played out. Sport and Emmitt both describe other cultures as loud or emotional. Although only Emmitt locates this quality in the body of an African American, Sport also ascribes loud and emotional behaviors to those he sees as different than himself. Delpit argues that many people focus on African American's "linguistic *performance* (what one does with language) belying linguistic *competence* (what one is capable of doing)" (52). In this way, the students locate strength in vocal characteristics, allowing the content of a message to go by without comment. The attribution of loudness to those of African descent is to recodify those bodies (and voices) as outside of the normal functioning of the classroom space. Even when coded as a compliment, the association still functions as a disciplinary move that otherizes the speakers of color in unique ways (Fordham).

Emmitt and Sport each located difference in the bodies and actions of only students of color, drawing on their paralanguage as the element of difference. This was similar to another pattern that arose in my interviews, in which students immediately identified students of color as the site of culture; when asked about culture in the classroom, students usually turned to students of color as their examples:

jtw: Did you notice any of the performances where you say people were trying to perform race in a particular way?

Keith: Well, when I saw Sydney, she always had stuff that is from her culture. You know, that she knows. Which is good and you can tell when she does it because she does it so well.

jtw: Have you seen anybody... I mean there's a lot of performances, especially during round one, where people were performing people who were not like themselves? People of different races?

Em: People who did what?

jtw: People from other races, so a lot of performances centered on that idea.

Em: Oh, yeah right. Frieda and Lakeeshia.

It is significant to note that when Emmitt and Keith were asked about enactments of culture in the classroom, they both offered someone of color, often naming the only people of color in the class. Students continued to locate difference via "culture" only in those performances by nonwhite people.

Stereotypes of African Americans are plentiful in the transcripts. While they often take the form of seemingly benign assessments like "loud" or "confident," they are just as frequently alluded to through the stereotypical adjective "ghetto." For example, in a class introduction, Marty, a white-appearing student, notes that she has "what they call a ghetto booty," slapping her behind for the class. The allusion is clearly to the stereotypes of African American women and the perception that they, as a class of people, have larger buttocks than white women. Thus, Marty's announcement that she has a "ghetto booty" is a clear reference to a cultural other, locating both her own rear end and, by extension, African American physiology as different, as culturally abnormal. In her study of "white trash" culture, Gael Sweeney argues that people get marked as other than white through excess. That is, white trash or people of color represent too much bodily matter. Thus, there is a lack of control, demanding a disciplinary marking of them as other, as excessive. The marking of black women by Marty in this way is a reiteration of whiteness's desire for control, for order.

Mollie, a white-identified woman, also constructs blackness through the "ghetto" metaphor:

> Mollie: Like, [softly] this is so bad, but I'm from Decatur and me and my friend one day, trying to figure out stuff we could say [that no one else could understand], 'cause he used to go to Millikan and we call it ghetto talk, 'cause it is—we come down here and nobody knows what we're talking about. And we're like, what? And I've broke my habit—I can't even think of stuff. But I'll go home for a month or two over breaks and stuff, and I'll pick up words and stuff and I'll be like "oh my God!" Stop talking like this! I sound so ignorant! And I think that's what it is, it's very distinct.
>
> jtw: How would you describe what ghetto talk is?
>
> Mollie: Let's see ... Just the way, in Decatur, the words you use like "salty" which means, has very meanings like don't you feel stupid. And in terms of fighting—it's like slang ... basically is what it is. But it sounds like Ebonics, which I don't think should be taking place, but ... I mean it is a form of language and a lot of people [pause] so ... I think that's the difference—a lot of people who aren't in that culture don't know those words, don't understand them.

Though appropriating a culturally loaded label, Mollie racializes the critique she makes of the language she and her friend created. In this way, she not only connects "ghetto talk" to blackness through the citation of Ebonics, thereby excluding herself from that group, but she also evaluates the talk as ignorant. Thus, whiteness becomes normalized through both race and class, as reflective of education. The connection to Ebonics is interesting as well, for as soon as ghetto talk is "like" Ebonics, Mollie's assessment no longer serves to describe the kind of speech, but performatively carries with it the criticism of black culture as well.

Emmitt also indirectly evaluates black speech in his commentary on a performance of "Hard Rock Returns to Prison from the Hospital for the Criminally Insane":

> Em: And, in the poem, it was written in Ebonics. And she tried to express Ebonics as well as she could through the play too, portraying black culture. That's what I noticed.

jtw: So, did you notice her heightening some of the language to try to make it seem like that? Is that how you got a sense of that? Or was it just in the reading?

Em: Yeah, 'cause... I particularly remember one point where she was like, they were talking about Hard Rock and they were, "you don't mess with that black mother—," you know? Or, "he's one mean son-of-a-bitch" or something like that. But there she really emphasized the Ebonics of the piece to represent culture, you know what I mean?

Emmitt does two things here that I think demonstrate the power of this kind of stereotypical construction of blackness. First, he locates Ebonics, as represented both in the poem and in the performance, as part of black culture, racializing the language style of the text. More important, he not only marks Ebonics as necessary in specific parts of the performance, but concomitantly marks the purity or neutrality of the language that surrounds it. In other words, the surrounding language (of the class, of the other parts of the poem, etc.) is unraced, unmarked, and uncontaminated. By constructing the poem's language in this way, Emmitt marks blackness as a linguistic contaminant. Second, Emmitt connects this form of language with the profane, citing only examples of "Ebonics" that include some kind of cursing. This way of representing black culture metaphorically connotes foulness (as in foul language). Here, blackness is stereotypically connected with dirt, implicitly otherizing Ebonics and those who speak it as somehow more likely to swear.

Classroom conversations also offered occasional chances for critique of racialized stereotypes. In one instance, Sydney notes: "I'm black. You are always going to be black. I grew up in a Catholic school. I didn't talk ghetto, but I'm still black. I will always be black." Sydney tries to undermine the stereotype that skin color equals ghettospeak, yet these moments are few and far between in the classrooms I observed, often being followed with some other stereotypical comment. Consider the following example from a class conversation about body art, in which Mora, an Indian woman who wears a nose ring, responds to another student who suggested body art as an element of culture: "I want to comment on the body art listed on the board. Some people from other cultures do stuff without knowing the significance of it. Like nose rings. They do it without knowing why, like it's fashion or just style." Schuyler asks, "Like your culture is being appropriated?" Sydney agrees, "Like white people getting dreads—they should leave it alone!" The class conversation continues on the subject of cultural appropriation. Connie states, "Maybe people pierce for different reasons. It's different for different cultures." Schuyler turns to Mora and immediately says, "Yes, there is that. We have to remember that." Then, Schuyler turns the conversation to another point and Mora sits back, remaining quiet for the remainder of the hour. This moment in class had the opportunity to radically challenge how students interacted with stereotypical constructions that lift up whiteness. By challenging the ability and the freedom whites enjoy to appropriate cultural symbols and rituals for their own use, these students could have done more to interrogate privilege. Yet, as soon as Schuyler accepts Connie's equalization of difference by sanctioning the unreflective appropriation of another's culture, she limits the possibility for subversion. Schuyler's turn to Mora in correction served to maintain the illusion of whiteness, making this student of color's own cultural experience undermined by the white teacher. Whiteness persisted in that space, even as Mora and Sydney tried to problematize it.

The use of stereotypes were plentiful in everyday conversation. And while there were occasional challenges, whiteness had the power to smooth the cracks, repair the damage, and solidify the foundation from which it asserts and builds itself. The normalization of whiteness built on the stereotypical constructions of nonwhites secures whiteness as the pure standard. Each and every time these stereotypes are offered without deconstruction, whiteness is reconstituted in all its authority.

Constructing Victimhood: "I'm not really entitled to any of my own opinions because they might offend someone else."

In the staged performances, some students worked very carefully to construct themselves as the victims, many times framing their own racial and social positions as at risk of being subject to the power of another. This also happened in everyday interactions, often occurring simultaneously with several of the other constructions of whiteness. For instance, when Ryan constructs her own feeling of difference as one of the "drama people" (see the section on sameness), she not only conflates style and race, but also constructs herself as a victim of difference, even as she reaps the benefits of white privilege. Such constructions of victimhood were less prevalent in class conversations and in interviews than most of the other constructions, but these performatives of whiteness are perhaps the most powerful. What could protect the sanctity of whiteness more than a claim to victimhood, demonstrating that one has been hurt or threatened by the very mechanisms that breed the white privilege on which such appropriations of victimage rely?

In her interview, Dallis constructs a very subtle construction of victimhood, framing herself as the arbitrator of cultural normativity—that is, she assumes the role of determining who gets to be the norm. However, she does so in ways that still allow her to claim victimization by the very people whom she marks as abnormal:

> Dallis: I don't know how the whole Texas thing came up. And we started talking about Minnesota and stuff like that.
>
> jtw: 'Cause in class—I think you even said people ... they were definitely not normal.
>
> Dallis: They're short. They're short.
>
> jtw: They're short?
>
> Dallis: They're short and rude.
>
> jtw: They're short and rude? Is that what makes them not normal?
>
> Dallis: That's the normal for them. [...] Like in New York, you could never see anyone open up the door for somebody or anything like that. And here it's like everybody holds open the door for everybody. [...] They would probably be offended or something or think that you are up to something. Or that you want something from them that they weren't going to give you. They seem suspicious then. I remember when we first moved to New York. Everybody would look at me and my mom because we were so tall compared to everybody else and it was just that they didn't know how to react to that. They were just looking at us like, "oh, great—*freaks!*"
>
> jtw: And how did you get the idea that they were thinking you were freaks?
>
> Dallis: I thought it was just the way they were looking at us and it was like, "how tall are you anyway?"

While Dallis' experiences in New York do not appear racially based, she nevertheless uses them to position herself as the victim of New York culture. What I find interesting is that this portion of the interview began with a discussion of what happened in class when students wouldn't talk about racial norms and instead would talk only about particular areas within the United States (see the section on contradictions). Dallis then offers this story, which places her under the watchful disciplinary gaze of New York culture. If she is the site of disciplinary mechanisms due to her outsider status, she cannot also be in a position of privilege. Dallis constructs herself as the object of discursive punishment even as she relies on white privilege.

Ryan positions herself with a similar victim construction:

It is almost like the southern, the southerners still make a big deal about the Civil War. I mean the whole confederate flag thing down in the south is a big thing and some schools still teach that we would have, we won the Civil War and all this stuff. And it's like, it's been over a hundred years since the Civil War and people are still talking about it as if it was yesterday and it's like, it's still a plight that needs to be dealt with. [...] Like when I moved to Tennessee from New York—whoa! That was interesting. That was a really big change, it was like, "oh, we have a Yankee!" And I actually, I never took it personally, but I'd make a comment in history class and everybody would be like, "*Shut up! You're a Yankee! Sit back down!*" [laughs] And I'm like, ugh! You know? It was like I was almost biased [toward], like, learning history because I wasn't born and raised in the south.

The above segment is a complicated construction of victimhood. Ryan locates herself as the object of attack by presumably white southerners, while also minimizing the possibility of her own implication in that critique. She begins by framing southern attention to the Civil War as an obsession—thus, she begins with the premise that all southerners place their energy on a misreading (the south really won) of a historical event. Ryan herself occupies the position of the reasonable white Yankee who is unfairly targeted and attacked by an obsessed cultural group.

In addition to locating herself normatively as the object of a symbolically violent discourse, Ryan's interview performance is emphasized by an increase in volume and intensity, underscoring that it is she who ultimately is the one who suffers condemnation. Then, rather than investigate or question why someone might challenge her, she undermines their critique by saying, "It was like I was *almost* biased" (my emphasis). She displaces their concerns by denying the possibility that she might be prejudiced. Again, her construction of herself as the reasonable, clearheaded northerner is juxtaposed to the irrational and violent other she has created. This positioning of victimhood, while not directly about race, works to position her as the object of oppressive acts. She never considers how she might be privileged or how this one system of power might be working within a larger discourse of racism.

Both Ryan and Dallis construct themselves as the subjects of exclusion, falling under punishing social sanctions based on geographical differences. If we place these two examples in dialogue with Karen, however, we see how the logic of victimhood persists in a more explicit form. Karen, describes what it means to be politically correct:

> Politically correct to me almost means that I'm not really entitled to any of my own opinions because they might offend someone else. So I have to pretend to go along with whatever the ideology of the day is so that no one is offended. And if I really disagree with something, voicing that disagreement is disrespectful to those who don't have the same opinion that I have. And, uhm, that for me is particularly frustrating.

jtw: Okay. Do you see a particular ideology being played out in Renee's class? So do you—Is there a culture there?

Karen: Oh definitely there's a culture in her class. [...] As a non-trad student, I obviously have a different value system than, than most of the kids in the class will have, where they go home in the evenings and go out to the parties or on the weekends their idea is going out and getting bombed, I go home and take care of children and do my studies and am involved in church activities and family activities and things like that, you know—I don't get to go home in the afternoon and study, I take my son to the orthodontist. And so it is a totally different value system and even lifestyle.

Karen couches her entire interview in a rhetoric that works to protect her privilege. Again and again she excludes groups of people, while all the time positioning herself as without the ability to voice dissenting opinions. She locates her outsider status in the class through her unique life roles: a nontraditional student ("I obviously have a different value system"), a Christian ("if I say anything about God, people will look at me like, oh yeah, you're one of those right-wing Christians, you know?"), and white ("it is almost going in the opposite direction now and we're getting reverse discrimination"). By naming herself as an underprivileged person, Karen constructs herself as a victim of political correctness. In her logic, the culture of political correctness renders her marginal in its effort to liberate or focus on others. Thus, she considers herself to be the one forced to give up her voice to make space for those who have the "loudest voices": "politically correct to me means that I'm not really entitled to any of my own opinions because they might offend someone else." Her identity as both white and victim is constituted in such a way as to secure her privilege. Her victimhood identity makes her helpless, unable to do anything about racism, since she is an unfortunate casualty of a politically correct system.

The critique of political correctness is not new, as James W. Carey reminds us, arguing that such a critique is an "effective political attack because it acts as a condensation symbol that names and coalesces growing resentments" against the leftist politics of cultural studies and higher education (58–59).[3] Karen's citation of political correctness is a strategic act that calls forth the power of a conservative ideology that masks differences without taking responsibility for the effects of such an effacement. In labeling herself a victim, she is again redrawing the boundaries between herself and those of a different race, again protecting self without regard for others.

In each of the above examples, these students strategically story themselves as victims, constructing their own whiteness as in danger and in need of protecting. Karen perhaps said it most powerfully:

> Karen: We're getting reverse discrimination. And as the mother of two white sons, that bothers me. Because I don't either a ...
> jtw: And that's discrimination against ... ?
> Karen: Against white males. And I'm not ... I can't prove this, but the quota system has set up a system whereby if I'm up for a job and a black woman is up for the job and we both have the same abilities, I can be reasonably sure that she is getting the job. Based on no other factor than that she is black and I am white. And I'm not sure that's fair to either one of us.

Karen sums up the danger of this kind of construction, placing white males, the most privileged social group, as the ultimate site of discrimination. By locating whiteness outside the center, placing it discursively on the margins, she reconstitutes the power of whiteness's position as the culturally pure and secured center. It is the ability of the privileged to claim they are equally oppressed as those who continually find themselves the subject of social inequality, while never accounting for their own complicity in that process. Karen, like the others, constructs herself as a victim, reinstituting whiteness's power to name, whiteness's power to continually constitute itself as privileged even through the claim of victimhood.

Constructing Whiteness

As I draw this chapter to a close, I am reminded of Kirk Fuoss' recent essay on lynching performances. While none of the examples in this chapter match the violence and physical injury of lynching, they are not without their brutal undertones. When Sydney, in the conversation about mascots, gets shut down, that is a violent act. Karen's desire to preserve her own privilege through attacking the other is a violent act. The repeated ideologies, the insistent efforts to protect the white cultural center, and the maintenance of cultural purity each function as subtle forms of violence by securing the status quo in ways that ensure that power remains in the hands of the powerful. It is the violence I see in many of these mundane enactments of whiteness that leads me back to Fuoss. He argues:

> My belief that awful as these particular performances were—and they *were* awful—they are best not forgotten. Remembering them, analyzing them, theorizing them does not necessarily mean that lessons will be learned. But forgetting them, avoiding them, ignoring them, almost certainly means that they will not. (29)

And while Fuoss is talking about historical acts, he is also talking about how these performances have effects that continue today, as evidenced by the lynching of James Byrd Jr. in 1998. So, too, do the performances I have addressed here—both on the stage and in everyday interaction. They are built from a historical legacy of racial inequality that gets preserved, reproduced, and normalized through the everyday dynamics I have studied. These performances maintain privilege—a mundane maintenance accomplishing whiteness.

Notes

[1] Karen's interview demonstrated many of the themes offered in this chapter. I discuss her here, as well as in the section "constructing victimhood" because Karen's discourse so clearly highlights the power of these two performatives. Karen's interview was very complicated, thus I have tried to demonstrate its power and hybridic nature by discussing it in these multiple contexts.

[2] See Miller for an extensive analysis of the performance of Native American images as mascots.

[3] Carey is one of several authors who wrote about political correctness, higher education, and communication in the 1992 spring edition of *Journal of Communication*. See also Asante's powerful analysis of PC discourse as hyperbolic, which nicely undermine such attacks against democratic pluralism.

Chapter Five

Ethical Reflections:
The White Researcher as a Performative of Whiteness

It was an average day in the site. My yellow legal pad rests on the desk in front of me, the date etched on the top in lead. I am sitting next to Emmitt, a student who has chosen the name of Emmitt Smith, a professional football player, as his pseudonym. Emmitt is a large young white man, wearing a "big daddy" T-shirt that says something like: "Warning: The consumption of too much alcohol may cause you to believe that you are actually bigger than I am." Emmitt likes to talk to me. He likes to talk to me before class, after class, and sometimes, much to the instructor's dismay, during class. But right now, it is before class and I like Emmitt, so I talk with him. He jumps from topic to topic, searching for something that might spark conversation. He begins with fishing. Emmitt likes to fish and often tells the class of his weekend trip to Campus Lake.

"Gross. Do you know how dirty Campus Lake is?" says Joel. Joel is one of my "favorites" this semester. He is an active class member, who was out of the semester for about three weeks due to a very bad automobile accident. In my notes, I call Joel "Joel (dh)." The "dh" is for dark hair since there are two Joels in the class, the other with very short blond hair (thus, "bh").

"No. The fish are really good there. I'll cook you up some. I've been eating those fish for years." Emmitt pauses, looks down at himself and continues: "And I seem to be doing okay."

I shift in my chair, turning to Emmitt: "So you went fishing this weekend?" Emmitt smiles and begins to narrate the subtleties of the weekend. Eventually, he talks about his plans for the next weekend. "I'm going to the Alan Jackson concert next weekend. Are you going?" I smile and note that I'm not really a country music fan. He laughs: "Well, I like all kinds of music: rock, metal, country. I like it all. What do you like?" I try to figure out how to admit to liking showtunes, with folk, pop, and light alternative on the side, when he begins to talk again: "Hey, are you going to do interviews still? Can I do one? I wouldn't mind doing one. That would be fun. I-I-I think that would be cool." Emmitt has a slight stutter, which he noted to the class during his first performance. I smile and tell him I am waiting until the end of the semester to conduct the interviews, waiting until most folks have been through the majority of the class. Then, the instructor waves for the class's attention, officially beginning her lecture, and I put pencil to paper and begin my daily notes.

As the class proceeds, I take notes on who says what—the everyday doings of the ethnographer. The class is discussing cultural norms—who is normed and who is not. Emmitt raises his hand, his body leaning over the right corner of my desk: "I want to be my own person—I don't want to follow anyone else," he says. I write this down, interested in the use of individualism and how that logic may or may not be an element of whiteness. Emmitt looks over at me. I smile, looking down at my notepad. The writing is only halfway down the page; Emmitt's name and the quote barely meet the second of three holes punched into the side of the tablet, but they stand out. As I look down at the pad, they appear to be the most easily readable things on the page—as if someone from the other side of the room could read it if they happened to glance this way. It seems to be like a bright sign—a neon notation that Emmitt said something that was worth my writing down. The light from the tablet's words, the brilliance of the mark I copied down illuminates the room and I feel as if my notes are disturbingly present—disturbing everyone.

Are they watching? Is Emmitt watching? It is so clear. It is so loud. It is so noticeable, this marking. I cringe and worry Emmitt will see it. Will he know that I wrote his name down? Will he care? Will he wonder why the comment Ryan made just minutes before didn't get written down? Was Emmitt's that much more interesting? Does he think that I think he is racist?—this is the nature of informed consent: They know I am studing race in the classroom and that I'm studying them. And here is this bright, so bright, so amazingly bright sign of marking, my marking, my marking of Emmitt, my marking of him in this way and he can see it. He can see it! How do I gain his trust for interviews and continued conversation when he knows I wrote this down about him? It seems so clearly a breach of his trust. I cringe again.

Then, I turn the page over, wasting half a sheet of notebook paper that will never feel the pressure of the lead pencil. I turn it over so he won't see, so the noise and the light and the mark will disappear. What Emmitt said is now hushed between the pages of the notepad, and when I look up, Emmitt is still looking at Lucy, still looking at the teacher. Then he turns to me, glances ever so slightly at the cleanliness of my notepad, not a mark on it, and then back to me, smiling. He turns to the instructor again. I sigh. Safe.

19 January 2000

Today is the first day of the semester, my fourth consecutive semester of fieldwork. I enter the room and twenty-five students sit in the hard plastic chairs and scattered desks that border the room. The room is familiar to me. It is a room that I have taken classes in, taught in, and for the third semester, will take notes in. The students glance up at me and I suspect they already know I am not a student. Thus far, I have yet to be confused with a student. I am unsure of why this is so. Am I so old? Do I carry myself somehow differently than undergraduates? I am curious what marks me as always already not them. But I don't ask. Instead I enter, nod at Lucy, and take a seat in the room. The class does several opening day activities: *Am I pronouncing your name correctly? How many performances? What are performances? Can you call me Steve?—I hate Stephen.* Finally, it is my turn to talk. The students turn to me as I begin.

"Hello. My name is John and I'm a doctoral student here in the department. I am studying performance and culture and would like to ask your permission to observe the class." I do my opening lines with as much enthusiasm as I can muster. In the back of my mind, I am reminded of human subject rules—everyone must grant permission for me to stay. A drop of sweat begins to drip down my back, sending a shiver through my body. "By signing this permission slip, you only grant me the ability to sit here with you this semester—you are not agreeing to anything else. Later, I may ask some generous souls for interviews, but right now I am just asking for your permission to observe." I smile nervously, knowing that this "informed consent" is giving them just enough information to get permission, not to really make sure they understand what I am going to do with their words.

Further, I wonder how much freedom these students feel right now. I wonder if they really feel they can say no, deny me access to their lives. I look at Lucy, sweet Lucy. She is the third teacher who has opened her

classroom to my eyes. How scary that must be. I wonder
if she felt she could say no. I am reminded of another
teacher who turned me and my research down, requesting
that his class not be involved. I am reminded of how
that strained our friendship. I am reminded of how much
people are willing to give up in order to maintain relationships. Today, I have entered Lucy's classroom with
the guarantee that it will be documented. I wonder if
she is suspicious of me. Maybe she is. Maybe she should
be. When permission is granted, each student signing the
white photocopied slip, I smile and thank them, wiping
my hand subtly across my forehead, trying to wipe away
my nervousness.

21 January 2000
    The second day is already playful; these students are
already beginning to grow accustomed to the easygoing
nature of Lucy's classroom. This classroom radiates energy, each student occupying space here in very nontraditional pedagogical ways. Rows give way to scattered
clusters in a rough circle that surrounds the perimeter
of the room, denying the educational naturalization of
rows. Students move freely in this space, often getting
up in the middle of a lecture or discussion to throw
away trash or exit for the restroom. Several students
sit on the carpeted floor, leaning onto friends' legs.
Andrew and Carla, two white-appearing students who I
discover are dating, often hold hands and lean against
each other. This place feels very different than last
semester, where the class I observed met in a more traditional classroom. The gift of space, this class enjoys.
    Toward the end of the hour, students discuss the dif-
ferences and similarities between "communication," "performance," and "culture." Lucy begins: "So, if everyone
is a performer, you can each do Hamlet?" The class
laughs a bit, Lucy making a face somewhere between a
smirk and a smile. Lakeeshia, a young African American
theatre student, shakes her head, noting: "Acting is
different than performing." The class continues and I

glance around the room. The students appear very in-volved, often making notations on open tablets.

As the conversation continues, the students begin to talk about culture. Andrew, a large, pale man with a shaved head, notes that "females are different than males. You know, if a guy gives me a piece of gum, you're a friend!" Frieda, a thin woman who has identi-fied herself in class as an African student who spent most of her time growing up in the United States, agrees, "We take things more to heart." Quickly follow-ing up on this, Tonya, a student of Greek descent, notes: "Females are more edgy." Lakeeshia shakes her head, "Women are more emotional." In response, Lucy asks, "Is gender a culture?"

Ken, a pale young man with trimmed red hair, answers affirmatively: "Definitely! I mean, it's like in the Middle East where women must walk behind. They can't even go in the same doors—the women have to enter the house from the back door."[1] The class nods, the conversa-tion continues, leading to where it always does, to the "We're All Americans" banner line. While usually it is the conflation of difference into a unified national identity that holds my attention, I am too caught up in Ken's comment to notice when Joan, the "We're All Ameri-cans" spokesperson this semester, says it. The quick critique Ken makes of gender practices in the "Middle East," the rapid and almost unified agreement amongst the class members demonstrated by head nods and the ab-sence of protest, and the easy shift into the next part of the conversation all trouble me. The ease at seeing problematic gender practices in foreign places is set against the myopia of their own conversation about the emotional state of women. I make a note on my own tablet wondering how this mix of race, gender, ethnicity, and nationality will play out for the rest of the semester.

24 January 2000

Joel (dh) notes in an introductory performance that he immediately went from his high school graduation to the military. "I'm a veteran—the Marines really

straightened me out. I had to join the military 'cause
my parents don't do handouts—I have to pay my own way
through school." I learn today that three men in the
class were in the military; two of them were in the
sniper unit. Another class member, Trish, was also in
the Army. Joel (dh) continues: "I'm a big brother to my
step- and half-siblings. I always try to push them into
athletics, but all they want to do is watch TV or play
on the computer. I try to push them to be the best, to
be independent." As Joel (dh) talks, his short-sleeved
shirt lifts a bit, revealing a large tattoo of an eagle
framed with his military troop name and unit number.
Joel (dh) carries with him a sense of confidence that
erupts in class, smothering the class in self-righteous,
pull-yourself-up-by-your-bootstraps ideology that stings
my own senses. I am again reminded that the conservative
myth of meritocracy is easy precisely because of its
commonsense place in the everyday discourses of our
lives. I don't like Joel (dh). Yet, I am amazingly attracted to his confidence, almost seduced by the power
of his rhetoric, the power of privilege radiating from
his every step. What makes this privilege all the more
intoxicating is the I-had-to-earn-everything-I-got-in-
life tone in his voice. I have to shake my head to pull
my stare away, to break his spell.

No, I don't like Joel (dh) at all.

31 January 2000

Lucy begins each class with a question of the day, a
technique used by almost each teacher I have observed.
Today's question: "The Super Bowl: Did you care? And if
so, who did you root for?" Answers vary, from students
who are heavily dedicated to the game to those who were
unaware it had occurred. Nate, a quiet, white-appearing
student who rarely talks in class, responds that he
"rooted for the Titans. I am so tired of seeing Kurt
Warner's ugly wife on TV." Several students laugh. I
don't know who Kurt Warner is, what his wife looks like,
or even whose team they are associated with, so I don't
laugh.

Laura laughs and asks, "Why is football 'football' here and not soccer?" Laura has a rich brown skin pigment, suggesting Latino or Native American heritage. Laura reminds me a great deal of Scott, a student from the previous semester, who also had darker skin, almost as if both of them have perpetual tans. Neither of them foreground their racial identities, neither talk about their race, often allowing race to be as absent (at least to my white eyes) as that of the white students.

Laura and Scott represent a tension for me as a researcher on race, because they remind me of why I use terms such as "white appearing" when describing students. This tentative naming forces me to always foreground my own location as a reader of culture and racial identities. I feel the pull of curiosity on my body, wanting to interview them for no other reason than to find out "what" they are—to diagnosis them and rest my mind, their race figured out and defined. Yet, I never did interview Scott, nor did I ever ask him to describe his racial identity. I know now I will not ask Laura either, for I really feel the desire to leave that question unanswered. To ask is to rely on some sort of "truth" that can somehow ease my curious mind. To ask is to put to rest a question that is itself more interesting than any answer I may ever get. It is to take the magical moment of not knowing and force it to some sort of resolution, relying on definitive answers: this, not that. To ask is to try to mend the cracks in the foundations of racial sedimentation that Laura and Scott somehow represent to me. My inability to say this or that tells me to question all the bodies I see in front of me, demanding that I search for the ways they make race matter.

Tom responds to Laura's question about the United States' use of the term "football" by stating, "Because America is stupid." Joel (dh) responds immediately: "Don't get started." It is not harsh or sharp, just definitive. Tom doesn't "get started," and class continues.

2 February 2000

Today is a class discussion on culture. Lucy has begun by writing on the board "Performance is ontoepistemic." "People are both makers and products of culture," she begins.

This semester has struck my body quite differently than the others. While I have been trying to read race in people's actions and talk, I have found myself growing more and more aware of many of the other ways students construct identity. Tonya gathers her books after class, pulls out a cell phone and calls her friend as she walks down the brightly lit hallway. It is a productive making of social class, the profit of economically privileged parents. Andrew and Carla are growing closer and closer, often touching in class, his hand on her inner thigh inches from her crotch, her head on his shoulder as they listen to lectures. This is a publicly allowed, socially accepted, and many times invisible heteronormative moment of bodies—his and hers—touching, the safety of sanctioned sex. Lakeeshia consistently cites God and Jesus in class and in performance, a prayer not silenced by this Midwestern classroom space. These markers of privilege, often just as ignored and passed over as the marking of race, rise up out of the fog of artificially naturalized invisibility.

Tim raises his hand. "There are bar cultures, you know? There are people who go to certain bars: Punch, Trez, RJ's. Club Quad definitely has a particular angle." The mention of Club Quad, the only gay club in town, starts conversation. Shelly, pushing her blond hair out of her heavily madeup, white-appearing face, adds, "I went there once. But I'm not gay!" She laughs, another reiterative act of heteronormativity dissipating into the air. Emmitt, a puzzled expression on his face, asks, "Is that what it is? I've never been there." His denial, his necessary statement of ignorance, his reiteration.

As we get ready to leave, I rub my eyes to erase the frustration built up there. I am the silent(-appearing?) observer. I am neither complicitous nor contradictory.

It has been a long day and I am ready to get out of here. Lucy asks for questions on the assignment. Frieda again asks Lucy to distinguish between a speech and a performance: "We read the poem and then give a speech on what it means?" Lucy smiles, though I can see frustration in her eyes. She repeats a description of the assignment, trying to answer a question Frieda has asked four previous times. Frieda nods slowly, her brow wrinkled. "Do we need to pick a culture totally opposite from us?" she asks, holding up the assignment sheet. Lucy shakes her head, "No, but it should be different than you in some way." Lucy turns her head and looks around, "Yes, Laura?" "Lucy? If we are part of a culture, but don't know anything about it, can we do that? I mean, I'm American Indian, but I don't know anything about it. Can I work on that for project one?" As Lucy confirms that she can, I grumpily slump in my chair, the generative ambiguity about Laura's racial identity somehow less meaningful now that I hear it spoken, now that I have an easy identifier, now that I have the privilege of smoothing over the cracks of my own questioning.

Part of the role of the ethnographer is to watch. It is to enter the site and watch others, record what they do, make sense of what they do, and then report it as a way of contributing to the field. One watches with a purpose. While I believe that some ethnographers enter with the purpose of allowing the site to speak for itself—to allow the research questions to formulate from their experience of the other, I entered my research site with the purpose of watching students talk about, embody, and then reflect on embodiments of race in general, and whiteness in particular. Regardless of the breadth or narrowness of the purpose, the ethnographer has an agenda. Ultimately, my agenda was to find enough "stuff" with which to formulate a substantial research project and, if I was lucky, to capture the stuff through writing in ways that would be interesting to others. I wanted it to be interesting to myself, to possible publishers and editors, and to those in performance and cultural studies who might read it.

With this kind of baggage, I went into the field and was surprised to find that I enjoyed the process. Like H. L. Goodall in his new book *Writing the New Ethnography*, I found that "living the ethnographic life [was] fun" (25). It was pleasurable to enter the classroom, to have students ask me questions, to be in

the presence of undergraduate life. I was the "other teacher." The other expert. Yet, I was also, in a limited but viscerally real sense, one of them. I performed with them. I talked to them before class. They asked me to repeat what the teacher had just said. And they would confide in me about what was going on in the class. They treated me, perhaps for the last time ever, as if I were one of the crowd. And that felt so good.

Each day of my research, I would gather my tablet and my folder and trot to class, sit in the midst of students, and take notes. As the pages gathered in the folder, as the firm edges of the folder wore tattered, as the computer printed pages and pages of fieldnotes, as the tapes to transcribe piled, I reveled in the ethnographic process. It was an active pleasure that I found myself caught up within and in it I stayed as long as I could.

The best days were the days I knew I had gotten "good" data. Those days—the days I got information that I knew would be featured in the book— lifted me up in ways that felt like a drug-induced high. I would go home, anxious to tell my partner of the day's events. Like a soap opera, I would tell what happened, saving the juicy bits to the end of the story. Those times when she sighed, asking "Really?" brought another high, another boost. Once, the teacher asked me what I thought of the day's class and I responded that "it was great— I got tons of good data for my project." When I realized that she was asking about how she handled the class discussion, I stepped back and noted it went well. Truth be told, I couldn't even remember what she had done. I was too caught up in the jewel of the day, the possible spotlight of the book.

4 February 2000
Today Lakeeshia has brought a sample performance for the class—a favorite poem of hers that she thought might provide the class with a workshop on how to create an aesthetic performance from nondramatic literature. She has memorized it, telling Lucy that she doesn't need anyone on book for her. Lakeeshia, the theatre major, is a young black woman with power in her voice. She moves into a pool of light in the center of the room. "Ego Tripping," she says and lowers her head, closes her eyes, and takes a deep breath. For a brief moment, it is still and quiet as the class grows more focused on Lakeeshia standing in the pool of light. A smile creeps onto Lakeeshia's face, her head rolls up, and her eyes

look through us. "I was born in the Congo. I am a beautiful woman. The hair from my head, gold and thin—I am
perfect." She continues, wrapping us up in the power of
her voice. Her gestures, her articulation, her welcoming
us into her performance make me think of the powerful
evangelical voice on my TV I pass through on Sunday
mornings, the image of the black preacher who carries
the word of God to the congregation. She speaks of di-
recting the rivers to flow, of building the mountains,
of the creation of the world—this perfect woman embodied
by Lakeeshia in a small pool of light.

When the performance finishes, the light returns to
full, and the room is back in the rough circle around
the sides of the room, Lucy offers the first compliment,
"Good job, Lakeeshia!" Many others offer compliments,
drawing images and quotes from the performance to support their points, *Wow, how articulate. There was a lot
of rage in there. She gave good meaning to her story—how
God made the universe. She's like Mother Nature. Definitely. Hey, who says God is not a woman? She has golden
hair. About the creation of people. We are the result of
all things done. She's confident. Yeah, confident.* The
voices overlap, creating a mingling of points and of
tones. I struggle to write them all down, wanting to
comment on them all. What does it mean to begin with
"articulate"? Do their comments carry with them an assumption of blackness and speech? If so, how? But before
I can really formulate that kind of response, I am off
to the next image—golden hair? This powerful black
woman, calling on a vocal style that is reminiscent of
black evangelical speech, has golden hair? What do I
make of Lakeeshia's choice to speak this poem, with the
ultimate image of white privilege—that golden hair—with
such a culturally loaded way of speaking? Or, more important, what does it mean that I immediately connected
a performance by a powerful black woman to that racially
specific production of religion? Is this connection her
or me? So much is going on here. My hand is cramping
with the writing.

Nate raises his hand, "I thought she was intimidating—she felt like that to me." Ken nods, "Yeah. You
know, I think it depends on how you were raised. I was
raised not to brag." Suddenly, my questions about how
Lakeeshia's voice resembles my perception of the exuber-
ant vocal style of African American preachers rubs
against Ken's perceptions of what it might mean to see a
confident black woman. We both rely on differing preconceived racial categories begging the question: What representations of female blackness do I have outside of
popular culture? Can I see Lakeeshia outside of those
acts, outside of those preconceived categories? How did
I just (re)create the very oppressive strictures of
black female identity without realizing I had done it?

7 February 2000

Carla treats today like "Show and Tell," passing out
Belgian money she received during a recent trip over-
seas. Carla is a seventeen-year-old first-year student,
who, I have learned, is "informally engaged" to Andrew.
Each day they enter the room together and sit on the far
side. Carla sits in a desk while Andrew pulls a chair up
close to Carla's right side. Andrew is a large muscular
man of twenty-five years, his shaved head punctuating
the presence of small circular eyeglasses which rest on
his nose. Carla's trademark thus far this semester is
her burping: *I burp*, she said one day. She allows a
pause to let that set in: *Loudly. Some girls look at me
and they are like, ugh! Some are cool.* But now Carla is
walking around the room showing everybody her recently
acquired Belgian coins and bills. After Lucy requests
that Carla tell the class about her trip, she picks up
the remaining bills on her desk, asking Andrew to get
the other coins out of her backpack, and turns to the
class. "Well, I went to Europe after graduation. I went
to Belgium first. There are some really mean people in
Belgium. They're all mean. Anyway, I think the money
really reflects how the people are. Portugal is really
traditional—the coins are really plain and boring." She,
searches for a sample coin amidst the pile in her hand.

"In Belgium, it is really full of culture and the money
has color. The money has lots of culture on it, music
and stuff. But the people are really mean. Uhm, like, I
was in this deli and I asked what the soup was and the
woman looked at me and was like, *over there!*" Carla
points behind her, reenacting what I assume to be the
server pointing to a sign. "Very mean," Carla says as
she passes around the coins. When she is finished, she
sits, leaning over to Andrew. He kisses her head and she
smiles.

11 February 2000

I am a bit nervous today. In the center of my stomach
is that familiar churning that comes with the preperfor-
mance jitters. Today I will perform for the class. This
is a service I provide to the instructors who so kindly
open their classrooms to me. I perform as a live example
and then answer questions from the students. I have prepared a piece by Leslie Marmon Silko entitled "Long Time
Ago," extracted from her novel *Ceremony*. I have spent
the last several days trying to bring the poem back to
my memory, not having had the opportunity to perform it
in several months. The class is settled now and I enter
the performance space. I have already adjusted the
lights, so I stand in the light centered in the middle
of the room. "Long time ago/in the beginning/there were
no white people in this world," I begin. I look directly
into the eyes of each audience member, trying to draw
them all into my story.

I have mixed feelings about doing performances in
front of these students, knowing that those who have
never performed before will usually have one of two reactions. On the one hand, they see me and realize that
this is something that they can do. *Oh! That's what we
have to do! I can do that!* On the other hand, they see
me, a performer of some ten or more years, and imagine
they will have to do what I do. *I can't do that. How did
he memorize all those lines?*

I finish the performance and I am invited to lead a
discussion on memorization and staging poetry. I enjoy

the opportunity to speak. Often I am quiet in class, going weeks without talking except to those willing to
talk to me before and after class. I feel a bit like the
teacher today, imparting advice and citing the textbook
for support of what I do to prepare a performance. When
the class is over I gather my materials, a bit sad that
the class period—my class period—is over. I look up as
Laura approaches Lucy. She is holding her book open,
pointing to what I assume to be a poem. All I hear her
ask is "What is the 'Trail of Tears'?" I shudder, remembering that Laura identified herself to the class as being of Native American descent.

Suddenly, I am angry. It hits me kind of suddenly and
I am unsure if it is the postperformance release of energy, but I do know I am angry. I am angry at Laura. I
am angry at her for not knowing about the Trail of
Tears. I am angry that she is asking this question while
most of her classmates are in the room, several notice-
ably watching the interaction, themselves waiting to ask
Lucy a question. I am angry at the implications of this
question: that someone of Native American descent
doesn't know, doesn't have to know, about the United
States government's slaughter of her ancestors as they
were marched off their land. And while she may know that
the deaths of her people occurred on some abstracted
level, the fact that she doesn't have the specifics of
this tragedy, the most noted and historicized example of
North American white colonialism, signals how widespread
and diffuse the seeds of whiteness are sown. And further, I am angry that white people will assume that if
she doesn't know, then *they* don't have to know. I am angry that her ignorance will let me and others like me
off the hook—history is just history, don't worry about
it! And while I know I am assigning responsibility to
her to know this historical violence as if only those
under white dominance are the ones who must remember it,
I can't help but feel angry. White folks in power often
elide the bodies of those they have tread upon, but that
same elision coming from those tread upon feels somehow
worse. I am angry. I am angry at Laura, even as I con-

sciously remind myself that this anger is a product of my own white privilege. Laura smiles and jokes with someone standing next to her: "I am Indian, but my sisters and I got lucky and got American first names." I pick up my papers and leave without waiting to talk to Lucy about the class. I am too angry. Too angry to stay.

And too afraid that in my anger, I might fail to remember that the ethnographer—this ethnographer—is to remain silent. So I leave and return to my office. With the door closed, I close my eyes and try to focus on the day's other tasks, knowing that it will be some time before I can concentrate on anything else.

14 February 2000

Valentine's Day. The class has rather low attendance today, reminding me of the pattern I've noticed during my research: People don't show the day before the first round of performances begin. As the class is still trickling in, Tonya smiles and asks Joel (bh) if he wants to hear a redneck joke. "You know you're a redneck if you hear 'hoe down' and your girlfriend hits the floor." Tonya, Joel (bh), and the two or three students who heard the joke laugh.

16 February 2000

The first day of performances are the most exciting for me. I love to enter the room and look around at the performers preparing their work. The students often sit looking through notes and copies of their selected poems. The room is electric with the physical energy produced by nervous bodies, anxious hearts, and queasy stomachs. I take my seat, a bit nervous on their behalf. I am sitting next to Dawn, a scheduled performer today. Dawn is poring over a tattered photocopy of Diane Burns' "Sure You Can Ask Me a Personal Question," occasionally pushing her light brown frosted blond hair out of her eyes. I like this poem. I like the voice articulating the text, the voice of an American Indian who, I think, carries justified anger at people who continue to refer to her through stereotypes. The mode of the poem lies in

a mysterious liminal space between direct address and a single-person narrative. That is, it can be staged as a conversation with an imagined other or it can be staged as a reflective, open narrative directed more to one's self. Dawn looks at the page, studying it, then lifts her eyes up, wrinkling her forehead as she mouths the words. Then, she looks down in either frustration or relief corresponding to her successful memory of Burns' lines. As the class gets under way, I watch her continue quizzing herself.

Dawn, however, is not the first performer. First, Frieda rises and begins to adjust the large wooden platforms, placing them snugly against the back wall, slightly stage left. She wraps a large silk scarf around her head creating a headdress, the cream, orange, and brown colors contrasting against her black tank top and black jeans. Her feet are bare as she climbs onto the platform and begins her piece. Softly from a stereo we hear African drums, the beat moving into Frieda's body. She begins to move to the music. "'Africa.' By Maya Angelou." It is probably the best performance of this poem I have ever seen, her dark body moving to the drums, creating scene, tempo, and persona with every ripple of her body. When it ends, the class applauds loudly. She smiles, embarrassed, and pulls her jeans up by the belt loops: "Sorry about my britches!" The class laughs at the break in the solemnity of the poem, grateful to find conversation in the aftermath of this experience. Frieda sits and begins to remove the scarf from her head. I scribble in my notebook, impressed with this performance from a first-time performer who has taken great risks on this first day of performances.

Dawn is next. She pulls out two chairs and places them in the pool of light left from Frieda's performance. She sits in the chair stage left and waits for Lucy to give the go-ahead. I see her mouth moving slightly and realize she is saying her lines one last time, one last chance to practice. I sigh, knowing that this will be a performance of Dawn talking to an empty chair. I think this is the least interesting reading of

this poem, but it often serves as a safe choice for those who are nervous and need an easy, straightforward poem. When Lucy smiles, nodding encouragingly to Dawn, she begins in a soft voice, the lines quietly aimed at the empty plastic chair. I grow curious at her voice, which is where Dawn has clearly spent time rehearsing. Her interpretation of the poem is carried in her vocal tone, thick with sarcasm. "No, I don't know where you can buy *Indian* rugs real cheap!" she says, drawing out the word "Indian" with pitch and a roll of the eye. Her face carries an almost ironic smile, as if this speaker is amused at the questions being asked of her. This persona is maintained throughout the performance, which ends with a laugh and a giggle: "That's it!" She bounds to her chair, leaving the chairs alone in the lights.

Again, I clap briefly and begin writing as much as I can about the performance. I am fascinated with this reading of the poem. Most readings of the poem I have seen shift the tone between a tired ironic sarcasm and anger. The persona in the poem reads to me as very angry, tired of all the insulting questions that get asked of Native Americans and their assumed life of alcohol-induced poverty. I am interested in Dawn's reading of this poem. Dawn was almost playful; at times looking at the empty chair as if these questions were so humorous, so unlikely, so out of nowhere, so unfamiliar. But the speaker I hear in this poem is not like that. The speaker does not sound confused by these questions, she sounds angry. The speaker lists responses one after another as if it were a mantra, as if it were a way to point out the incessant questioning that she encounters because of who she is, because of her race. The speaker is not playful. Who is it that can read this speaker as playful? Is this a misreading? If so, is the interpretation an element of Dawn's youthful age? Is it because of Dawn's whiteness? Is it because only someone privileged by the invisibility and perception of normalcy can elide the pain of this speaker's experience? I wonder what makes for this lightening of the speaker, a softening and erasure of the speaker's frustration. I wonder why

Dawn made this choice when so many others were possible.
After a minute of open discussion, Tom notes that Dawn's
performance "was cool. I love the sarcasm. It's like a
weird twist on Forrest Gump." He smiles, picking up his
backpack in preparation for the end of class.

I close my eyes. This persona was reduced to Forrest
Gump. I groan under my breath and begin to write down
Tom's comment. As I do, I hear Ken ask Frieda, "Are you
a dancer Frieda? There was someone in my Theatre 101
course who did some dancing—was that you?" Frieda raises
an eyebrow. I can almost hear what she might have heard
in that question: *Yeah, I saw this black person once who
danced and, since you're black and you dance, was that
you?* It is as if all people of color are the same. Ken's
white eyes conflate them into a single image of the
black dancer/athlete/entertainer. They are each there
for his viewing pleasure. I realize I am projecting this
onto Ken, onto Frieda, onto Dawn. I realize I am projecting a great deal here, but I can't seem to reel in
my thoughts. I close my eyes again and prepare to leave
as I hear Lucy excuse class for the day, reminding folks
of who performs the next class meeting.

18 February 2000

My thoughts of Dawn surround me as I reenter class
today. I am surprised at how worked up I get when I'm in
the class. I get so passionate and so judgmental in the
moment. I leave the class many times angry or annoyed at
the ways students are shaped by and continue to shape
whiteness. Yet almost as soon as I leave the classroom
and calm down in my office, I begin to write about it. I
take extensive notes and type up extensive narrative accounts, mixing commentary with "objective" accounts of
what happened. I can't separate the "what happened" from
the "and this means." They blur as soon as they hit the
page.

By the time I got home on Wednesday, Dawn had become
a fascinating tale—I told my partner over a chicken and
rice dinner what happened, noting the significance. My
excitement grew until I could no longer stand it and had

to stop, my grateful partner returning the conversation to the more mundane dinner talk of schedules and shopping lists. Later, in my office, the story began to pour out of me, the typos from my furious fingers making an almost incoherent jumble translatable only to my eyes. The voices in those performances are engraved in the memory of the computer for later use. I think this as I enter the room and see Dawn sitting with Mollie. I hear Mollie complimenting Dawn. Dawn nods her head, shaking her umbrella, which is dripping from the heavy rainstorm outside. I smile. I am unsure what the smile means. Does it mean that I am glad that she is receiving support? That the performative citation of whiteness in the performance gets affirmed, thus continuing to make a field for me to study? That I get to remain the only one who knows? I smile. And it scares me.

My thoughts are interrupted by Joel (bh). His richly tanned face, highlighted by his buzzed blond hair, has a thin film of sweat on it. He is pacing, pulling on a light brown silk tie that is draped down the front of a finely pressed white oxford shirt. His trim muscular figure is both obscured and illuminated by this attire, his wrinkle-free tan pants make a slight swishing sound as he paces almost directly in front of me. Lucy enters and Joel (bh) immediately tells her, "I have to go last! I have such a hangover, you don't even know!" She smiles and pats him on the shoulder, telling him he must negotiate with the other performers.

When it's Joel (bh)'s turn, he jumps up, clearly nervous. He tosses his papers into Lucy's lap, crossing to the area of light in the center of the room. He jumps up and down, shaking out energy. "My title is, 'Why did I get drunk last night and go to my 8 A.M. class?'" He laughs, his dimples deeply engraved on his smooth, evenly tanned face. "Actually, it is 'Sure You Can Ask Me a Personal Question,' but I am doing it differently than Dawn did. Have any of you ever said, 'Yeah I've got this black friend' or something? Well, I guess it can be anything really—religion or something. Anyway, I think this poem is about all those dumb questions you get when

you are just a bit different." He pauses, jumps up and
down again for a few seconds, takes a big deep breath,
and then begins.

I realize I am smiling again. Did he just do that? He
has just framed his performance of a poem on Native
American issues by detailing his abuse of alcohol. He
just jokingly titled the piece, 'Why did I get drunk
last night'! What does it mean for him to cite that performance of excess in relation to a cultural group that
has historically been marked with and by such abuses.
Regardless of intention, Joel (bh) just reiterated a
violent naming, re-creating his own privilege through
the association of his abuse with that of Native American culture. I am writing very fast, the pencil lead
making a soft but harsh noise as it inscribes my paper.

I look up and see him still smiling, struggling to
remember the lines of the poem. In the distance I hear a
crack of thunder and again, note, the storm brewing outside. Joel (bh) smiles: "No I didn't make it rain last
night." As Joel says this line of the poem, a huge roll
of thunder shakes the room and several people jump.
"Well, I did today, but not last night!" The class
chuckles at the additional material inserted without
pause into the performance directly one beat after the
thunder. I look around, advance the lead in my automatic
pencil, and continue to write.

21 February 2000
The first performer today is Tom. He undertakes what
I find to be a rather difficult task, choosing to perform Thomas' "Next Life, I'll Be White." This is a nonfiction piece about living as an African American in a
world that privileges whiteness. It is a powerful piece.
Tom, who complimented Dawn's choice of sarcasm, also
frames his piece with a thick layer of cynical humor. In
the talkback session, Tom notes that he was drawn to the
"outrageous" stories in the piece, noting that while
some were a "bit much," he still felt the piece was important: "It gets to me, you know? We are working toward
equality, yet it seems so far away. I know he sounds an-

gry in places, but I chose to underplay the anger and go with the sarcasm."

23 February 2000

Nate wears a dark blue long-sleeve T-shirt and baggy blue jeans. His brown hair has that tousled look, short and highlighted blond on the tips. He adjusts small wire-rimmed glasses as he waits for Lucy's cue to begin. "Today I'm doing 'I Think the New Teacher's a Queer.'" He lets out a small giggle. I am unsure whether this is to signal his discomfort performing or whether it is about performing a piece about queerness. He clears his throat and continues, "I chose it because the title was blunt and amusing, because it shows one minority's feelings on another." 'This is a confusing introduction,' I write under Nate's name. Nate sits in a desk he has placed in front of the chalkboard and begins the performance, whispering the title line toward the chalkboard. He immediately gets up, taking the persona of the teacher narrating a series of adolescent experiences brought forward by this comment. The poem Nate has chosen is horrifyingly violent, as the teacher-persona relives moments of violence on his body due to suspected violations of sexuality norms, all while now realizing that he is again in danger of being a target. This is how I know the poem, but this is not the poem I meet in Nate's performance. Nate stands at the chalkboard, his arm bent 90 degrees at the elbow, his relaxed hand swaying every time he shifts his weight. As he speaks the words of the teacher-persona, his deep voice is lifted an octave with a lisp twist. In overly feminine movement, Nate transforms this poem into a carnival, his othering of this character into a joke, subject to our heteronormative eyes. Several of the class members laugh openly at Nate's performance, now a reinstigation of violence on queer bodies, now an affirmation and protection of heterosexual privilege. When he finishes, Laura leads a loud ovation for the performance. I notice that several members of the class are not clapping, are looking toward Lucy, who herself is wearing a face of both

shock and disappointment. Nate smiles, lifting his left
hand to cover his mouth, his wedding ring glimmering in
the bright glare of the track lighting.

The class ends with a discussion of the performance,
asking Nate to justify the use of humor in such a violent poem. Nate realizes he has erred; Lucy isn't smiling. I imagine Nate will apologize to Lucy. She will
grade him and take into account the effect of his representation, his creation. He will try to explain it away.
He will probably feel bad about it all. I imagine all
this will happen, but now, that image is out there—Nate
at the chalkboard, the sound of the lisp, the presence
of the not-me wedding ring, the loud clapping of Laura's
hands, the surprised look on Nate's face when he realizes that not everyone liked it, and the new knowledge
that this place is not safe, was never safe, will never
be safe for all.

25 February 2000

Andrew sets up his performance space by placing a
large table in the center of the room and sitting behind
it in a black plastic chair. "I'm going to perform in
the dark, without any lights, because I think the words
are so powerful, I want you to use your imagination." He
begins R. T. Smith's "Red Anger," a short poem about
growing up in poverty on an Indian reservation. He keeps
his voice so soft, so barely audible, that the room is
literally leaning forward in their chairs, straining to
hear him. I can see by the thin line of light from the
door frame the bodies straining toward the sound of his
voice. The persona describes his brother choosing to
kill himself by shooting himself in the head. Andrew's
soft voice begins to grow during the stanza as he tries
to build the idea of rage. Suddenly, Andrew lets out a
monstrous scream—a scream so powerful that the force of
it pushes us back into our seats, caught off guard. I
stop writing, my head pops up in shock. Andrew, in a
cloak of darkness, stands, his chair falling backward
with a dry hollow plastic smack. Andrew screams again,
grabbing the underside of the table and tossing the

heavy mix of wood, metal, and plastic into the air as if it weighed no more than a few ounces. Through the darkness I see the table circle itself once. Then twice. It finally lands on one set of legs, the sound of bending metal screeching loudly in the room. Then, almost as suddenly as it began, the table falls over with a loud and final thud. The front row of the audience, many of whom are sitting on the floor, gasp as the table lands just feet from their own outstretched legs. In the deafening silence left after the explosion, I hear Andrew circling the room, breathing hard. Suddenly, he begins to laugh. "I just forgot my line," he says. The room lets out a nervous laugh, glad to have a release of the energy left from the crash of the table. When the lights are brought back up, several students investigate the thrown table—its two front legs drastically bent under the force of the fall. As four students struggle to remove the table from the room, Andrew smiles and tells Lucy that he "didn't mean to break the table."

Other than the reckless endangerment of the flying table hurtling at the audience and the burst of laughter that destroyed the moment, I am surprised by how much I like the performance. The power of the poem, the build of the tension to a powerful and unexpected climax, as well as the shock and discomfort, seem to capture the pain of the speaker. This is a performance that will dwell in me for some time.

What will also dwell is the fact that this white man destroyed property, endangered the well-being of classmates, and exercised violent anger in class and really was never held accountable for those acts. I wonder what that says about white privilege?

The first time I entered an ethnographic site I was excited. It was a combination of nervous butterflies in my stomach and an overwhelming sense that once I did this—once I entered, I would be forever changed, no longer innocent. My first time, I was well aware of the masculine nature of what I was about to do. Ethnography, by its conceptual design, is about entering, penetrating, breaking into the other in order to get what one wants. The site—that ethnographic other—is the land of plenty. It is there to be taken, to be consumed, to be tamed. The first time I knew I had gotten something good—some raw data, rich with the taste of academic success—I knew that ethnography was, for me, about sex. It was about entering into and returning, fulfilled. It was about watching the other, becoming the voyeur. How sensual it was to watch the bodies of those others, to make them exotic, to make them the subject of a gaze filled with the eye of consumption simply because they were not you, to make them the object of my gaze. They are there to be examined. Ethnography was sexy business.

I found the idea of being an ethnographer powerful, entering the site and rubbing against others until you reach ethnographic climax, until the ethnographer erupts in an academic epiphany that culminates in that authoritative sense of "being there." The ethnographer struggles, putting himself/herself in the midst of those others in order to be seduced by their language, their bodies, their performances. S/he seduces their stories, their experiences, their secrets for his/her own use. And through this seduction, the ethnographer in the site becomes sexy. Further, s/he grows only more sexy in the afterglow—the shift from gatherer to storyteller. The ethnographer becomes the one who knows... and tells. And doing this work, this ethnography, one becomes sexy in the academy. You then become the one in the locker room, telling the others of your conquests. You seduce those others through the telling, the wishing they were you. The ethnographer is not just any old researcher. As the ethnographer, you are sexy—you do ethnography. You get to become the object of others' gaze. Oh, I get goosebumps just thinking about it.

I've seen it—this power, this appeal, this raw display of intimate knowledge. To hear the ethnographer tell his/her stories, to momentarily be taken up in that scene, to be included in that tale, felt so sexual. Once, at a conference, I heard an ethnographer tell about traveling to Africa, wading through the moisture of the African wilderness, and I was so turned on. His lips, the lips of the ethnographer, spilling that moment on me like cool water from the tip of a long garden hose on a hot day. And I was drenched in his spray.

Confession time: I have never been sexy. At least, not before I was an ethnographer. I was never the football star, the most popular, the kid who got to sit at the cool table in the cafeteria. I was never sexy and I knew it. But I so wanted to be, to be sexy. I have never wanted anything as much as that. I have never desired anything more than to feel the pleasure of being, knowing that I was, seeing others' knowing looks that I was, definitely, sexy. To be sexy—this I wanted. More than anything.

But then I met ethnography, and for the first time felt sexy. It started in my stomach, this nervous sexiness, and spread up and down throughout my entire body. I felt sexy in ethnography, as the ethnographer. I could enter the site and people knew—I think they knew I was sexy there. And even if they didn't, I knew. I knew I was finally sexy. Then, the first time, with virginlike excitement, I told someone what happened in the site. And there, in the look on their face, I could see that I was sexy. Finally sexy. I was, for the first time, the storyteller in the locker room. The more exciting, the more appalling, the more vivid, the more thrilling the story was, the more sexy I felt. I am seduced by ethnography, and through that seduction, I offer myself and my tales for others to be drawn into my allure.

I am an ethnographer.

And ethnographers are sexy.

So very, very sexy...

3 March 2000

After a long absence, Joel (dh) has returned to class. When the questioning students ask where he was, he admits that he was out due to a serious accident in which he flipped his Jeep several times, causing some minor head injuries. "I'm fine now. The thing that's really depressing is that I was selling the Jeep and now it's not worth much. In fact it's totaled. Now I have no Jeep and no money." He smiles; the class quietly looks at Joel (dh) as if searching for clues to his accident, a hint at the damage.

Quickly the class begins discussion on the next assignment, which centers around performing cultural themes through the creation of a compilation, or intertextual, script rather than working on a single poem or essay. Lucy asks the students which themes in the textbook stood out for them and, after much prodding and several minutes of silence, Lakeeshia notes that family caught her attention. "What makes a family?" offers Lucy.

Lakeeshia notes that family "means more than just immediate family—it can be like sports and churches."

Ken nods, "You need love and trust. You know, Joel could have died in that accident. We all laughed when he told us, but it was more serious. People don't care anymore. We are raising some uncompassionate children."

Joel (dh) immediately responds. "I left home at seventeen—I've been on my own for a long time. I like to stand on my own. I got these balloons and flowers after the accident. These folks would come to see me and I'm like, you don't even know me! Get out of here!" The conversation continues, but I am stuck on Joel (dh)'s adamant stance on his ability to stand on his own. The accident, the loss of his Jeep, and the near death experience all somehow seem to support his rugged, tough, give-me-what-you-got kind of persona. I don't know much about Joel (dh)'s life. I'm not sure of his family background other than that he is paying his own tuition through the GI Bill and that he is a big-brother figure in his family, pushing his siblings to succeed at all costs. This is a powerful spokesperson for the conservative ideology of meritocracy. He is the Republican dream—he takes a licking, blames himself, and then picks himself back up and keeps going.

"You know," begins Andrew, "the biggest family I've ever had is the military—they got your back for you. There's no shared values, just shared rules!"

The Joels nod in agreement, both of them adding to the conversation. "They're some close friends!" "They are brothers more than my real brothers."

Lucy offers a connection to the other students, "Does college breed the same kind of relationships? They both seem like an experience of dislocation."

"Totally not!" bellows Joel (dh). "I don't want to take away from any others, but in the military you have no choice. Everybody did the same thing. You don't have a choice—you do it. Here, I can stay in bed if I want and not come to class. Not in the military!" Andrew is nodding vigorously.

Dawn tries to enter the conversation, drawing a connection to her sorority. "I've lived in the dorm and they all want to hang out in the dorms. But I didn't want to—I wanted to go out. They thought I was a bitch so I left and joined a sorority. My best friend is in my sorority."

Joel (dh) is all over that. Mocking her, he says, "People ask me if I want to join a fraternity. Hell, I've been in the ultimate fraternity!" Andrew laughs. Their laughter continues for only a couple of seconds and I realize that it makes me kind of scared. I see these three faces—the Joels and Andrew—laughing. I want to find a way of talking about this moment, about their faces, about that laughter. What scares me is that when they laugh, it is the same laugh. You can't tell one voice from the other. It becomes so unified, so blurred that I can't tell who starts it or who ends it. And in those moments, the erasure of the Joels and Andrew—the making of this single laugh that has no name, no separate voice—I grow worried that my questioning voice might just very well break under the weight—under the weight of such powerful assertions built from privilege, under the weight of this discourse without anyone necessarily there, under this unified voice.

22 March 2000

The students have begun preparing for the second round of performances. The Joels have decided to pair up and create a performance about brotherhood in the military. "Hey Joel!" calls Joel (dh), "Do you have a belt? My blues fit, but I need a belt." Joel (bh) nods, "Yeah, I got one. Hey, Lucy? Do we get extra credit if we come in our Marine Corps blues?" They laugh and continue talking about what they will do in performance.

I look over at Andrew and Carla. Carla has missed several class meetings lately and it has come out in class that she is pregnant. Now, Carla is talking about her and Andrew's wedding, often bringing bridal magazines to class. She often invokes her impending wedding in class examples, as a citation of ritual, family, beliefs, culture, or anything else that will allow her to talk about it. Today, Carla is not feeling well, apparently from morning sickness. She leans her head on Andrew's shoulder; he pats and rubs her leg, allowing his hand to rest on her inner thigh.

The class discussion, now well under way, begins to address empathy in the performance process. Lucy tries to steer the class toward an understanding of the text— that through performance we can gain a greater empathy for others. Joel (dh) again turns to the Marines as his connecting example. "I think in the Marine Corps the three of us might have had the same experience. But everyone has the same experience—that's how you become so close. There's no taking the easy way out."

The class continues, moving among different people's examples of situations in which they felt empathy for someone else. Joel (dh) notes that "people don't react the same to all situations. If someone who was rich was in an accident, they have no idea what I'm going through. I can't just buy a new car."

Ken nods, "I couldn't be in the military. I would crack. People can have *similar* reactions, but not the same. You have to take into account a person's makeup."

Joel (dh) sighs. The class stops, looking at him. "You know, empathy can be bad. Sometimes I don't give empathy—these people use this stuff as crutches and I'm not one to help someone stay down. I'm in debt up to my eyeballs, but I'm just glad I'm up walking and talking. Get over it! Keep going! You know? I can say I know how you feel. I can listen. But then say I did this and I overcame it and now you can too. I hate weak people. They make me sick. I'll listen, but after a while, I'll just stop listening and say *enough*."

He continues, but I lose my ability to hear. I lose my ability to keep writing. Yet his voice keeps coming, keeps crashing on me, keeps forcing me under. "They look for help and never do anything to help themselves. Some of them are just leeches." My head swims, my vision blurs. I am lost in a sea of pull-yourself-up-by-your-bootstraps rhetoric. The waves hit me, the ebb and flow, the constant barrage of that voice. My head swims until I can't, keep writing, can't keep this up. I close my

notebook, look at my watch, and think… about… something…
else.

22 March 2000 (later)

I have woken up from a dream. It was in two parts. In
the first, I am standing in a pool of light surrounded
by dozens, maybe hundreds, of faceless voices. They
shout at me and I duck and cover my head with my arms.
*These people use this stuff as crutches and I'm not one
to help someone stay down.* The voices hurtle. Overlapping. Repeating. Growing louder, louder, louder, so much
louder. *Do we get extra credit if we come in our Marine
Corps blues?* I see the bodies surrounding me, but they
are in the shadows. They are faceless, just voices, just
discourse, just constant chiming, constant yelling, constant voices. *There's no shared values, just shared
rules!* I try to speak, but I can't hear my own voice. I
can't hear myself. *I hate weak people.* I try. *Some of
them are just leeches.* The voice, all one pitch, all one
volume, all the same, overpowers me. *They make me sick.*
And I crumple under the weight of that discourse. I
fall. And I know it's my fault. I did this to myself. I
let myself down. And I cry. Broken on the floor because
I did not have the strength to stand, I cry. And it's my
fault.

In the second part of the dream, I am on the Phil
Donahue show. The yellow and orange stripes from the
late seventies proudly sketch out Donahue's name. I look
up and see the lights from cameras and stage lights. I
think I see people in the audience, but their faces are
obscured, they are without definition. To my right is
Donahue. He is standing on the second and third steps of
the platform, holding a silver microphone trailing a
thick black cord that disappears into the blackness beyond the lights. "Today, we have Professor Warren," says
Donahue. I look around and then realize that he is re-
ferring to me. I smile. "You have written about the cultural power of whiteness. You have written about how
students enact whiteness in the classroom. In one very
interesting section of the book/article/chapter, you

have discussed how the logic of the military, what you call the 'myth of meritocracy,' helps perpetuate whiteness. Can you elaborate on this, as it was so clearly articulated in your book/article/chapter that nicely balanced the ills and benefits of this organization without using cheap, easy outs?" He bows his head, leaning forward onto his left knee, his microphone thrust toward me. "Well …" I begin, but I can't find the words. "Well, I think …" There is nothing I can say, so I sit and am swallowed up by the silence. And it's my fault.

And then I woke up.

29 March 2000

I enter the classroom, feeling the pressure of the middle of the semester. I am preparing for a conference in the next several weeks and have realized that I will miss several performances in the next round. I grow grumpy with the knowledge that this round is rich for analysis and I will be missing two days' worth of data. I wonder if I will miss the Marine day. Silently, I hope I will and wonder what that says about me. When I walk through the propped open door, I walk into a conversation already in progress.

Joel (bh): "Hey, Joel, are you pimping?"

Joel (dh) is wearing a tie and dark slacks. His tie nicely knotted at his neck, he returns the call. "It's hard to pimp twenty-four seven."

Joel (bh): "How about you, Laura? I'll give you two cents more than he gives you now!"

Laura smiles, her thin body barely covered in a small brown skirt and silk cream tank top. A thin line of Laura's mocha skin shows when she lifts her hand up to her chin, as if to consider the proposition. "Two cents, huh?" She laughs.

Joel (dh): "Ooohhh!" [He draws out this sound for several seconds.] "You'll be making a dime now!"

This interaction is ended when Lucy enters, and the participants each retreat to their seats smiling. I spend the rest of the hour thinking about this brief moment of play, this brief moment of consensual teasing.

Clearly, this moment is misogynist, the man-pimps bidding on the whore, offering her bits of money for her sexual service. Even as she willingly plays with them, the men do not treat her as an agent with the ability to really make decisions about her sexuality. Even as she considers the different offers, her status as the sexual object is never questioned or troubled. In effect, her decision is only one of a limited number of options possible, each of which has her selling her body for the profit and pleasure of men. But, this reading is complicated by race. Laura is not just a thin attractive female in the middle of two boys' play—she is a woman of color being bid on by two white men. I envision their inspection of her, their bids, and their profits. I shudder as I think about the historical mirroring of slave trading, the body of color sold to the highest bidder. This exchange, this white talk at the expense of Laura's body, serves to protect those who bid from those who are bid upon. Who has the privilege to name the whore? And who is subject to that naming? *This* is privilege.

12 April 2000

I have arrived in class to find that I missed the Marine performance. There is no tape, no access, no residue to smear across my notes. I make a mental note to ask Lucy about it and turn to the day's performances.

Carla and Andrew have already prepared the space. A table is along the back wall; a stool, alone in a small area of light, rests downstage. When everyone has settled, Carla begins. "On May 12, 1981, Carla was born into a two-parent household. My parents didn't love each other, but got married because they got pregnant with me." She continues, discussing how she grew up with her dad's values but didn't accept them. "I went to a white minority high school. It wasn't honors, which increased the minority population. I was the minority but I didn't care. It was cool." She gets down from the stool and crosses to the table where Andrew is waiting. They perform a bit out of the textbook, dramatizing a short

story about a white married couple discussing interracial marriage. In it, the woman asks the man, who is not
in favor of races mixing, what he would have done if she
were black—would he still want to be married to her?
They go back and forth until Andrew throws down a dish
towel he was holding and says, "Well, you're not
[black], so let's drop it!" He walks to the stool and
begins to address us just as Carla did before. "I was
born and raised in a family where we were taught to respect others. Raised not to look at skin color but in
their heart." Andrew's voice is shaking. He turns to
Carla, asking her to come over to the stool. Carla looks
confused and I suspect this is not in the script. She
sits on the stool, Andrew drops to one knee, and addresses her. "I love you. I see into your heart. I want
to spend the rest …" he continues, eventually proposing.
Carla says "yes," the class claps loudly, some whooping
is added to the mix. The rest of the performance that
Carla was waiting for back behind the table is no longer
possible; the applause signals the end.

    I lower my head, uncomfortable at this private moment
publicly displayed for the class. This performance of
heteronormativity washes over our bodies. Only I sense
its weight in ways that I have not before. And that
weight, aided by my own relationship with someone of the
opposite sex, is more easily carried. I wonder whose
body in this classroom, whose queer body, must add this
classroom moment onto his/her back, without the support
afforded by heterosexual privilege.

When one studies something, it is important that one find it, especially if
the presence of that thing is the basis of one's research. I came to my topic because I truly feel that my work might help illuminate how whiteness manifests
itself in the classroom and how whiteness breeds racism, exerting and maintaining power relations along that axis of power. I believe strongly that the study
does just that—it opens up the ways whiteness comes to matter. Yet, in doing
that work, I many times failed to register how such an exercise of this ethnographic research locates the subject of the project, how it locates me. As the
ethnographer, the pages of this text are my story. It is my attempt to make

sense of what happened during my two years in the introductory performance course "Performing Cultures." I have crafted it, pulling and relying on some moments, discounting others. There are multiple stories in my notes, in my transcripts, in my memory that will not be told. At least not told within the pages of this text. The story, as I unfold it, is about racism in production, manifested from the bodies of the participants in the study but told through my voice. A voice that gets high from seeing racism happen in front of me.

Imagine an ethnographer entering a site to find racism. Imagine him/her spending two years in the field, only to report that racism did not occur. Is this ethnographer happy? Does this professional sit back and joyfully report that the heart of racism has beaten its last beat? Does *that* get published? As an ethnographer, the days I left the field with a fairly empty tablet, finding little to write down about how these members talked about and embodied whiteness, were the lowest days of the project. And yet, the days when I saw moments of racism—from the minor citation of the rhetoric of color blindness to more gross examples of bitter racism demonstrated through racial slurs—were the days I left smiling. What does it mean to be a researcher who finds pleasure in the demonstration and perpetuation of racism? What does it mean to know that the jewel I find in the field, the spotlight moment in the book, is a reproduction of power lifting up my own cultural privilege on the backs of those nonwhites who suffer the weight of my whiteness? What does it mean to take joy from finding racism in the field? What kind of sickness is that?

17 April 2000
    Lucy begins by asking which performances people liked best this round. Ryan, an athletic white university cheerleader, offers the first response. "Andrew and Carla. 'Cause of the proposal."
    Lucy returns, "What was the performance about?"
    Ryan: "It was about how if one of them had been different, would they still be together."
    Lucy: "And what was that thing?"
    Ryan: "The color of their skin."
    Lucy spends several minutes trying to get the audience to see how the proposal may have undermined the message of the performance. The added proposal, which did little to help us understand the piece of literature

or the personal narratives, only outshone the message of the theme. The class nods.

I am fascinated by two things here. First, I do not find it incidental that Ryan doesn't say out loud that the difference between the couple in the performance was race. That element seems very strategic—by not naming the difference, Ryan masks the element of race and thus the racial politics of interracial dating and marriage. The story would not have been the same if they had been talking about hair color or height—it relied on the whiteness of the speaker's bodies and the factor of race as the contaminant. Yet, Ryan's elision of race as the defining element of the husband's decision to marry or not obscures the racialization of the story, generalizing the concerns about race to anything. This elision does not seem incidental at all.

However, the second point here that needs examining is the fact that the proposal, which Ryan credits with being the element of the performance that made it the "best," was between two white people. This also was not incidental because the whiteness of Andrew's proposal trumps any resistance generated by the performance. By making that proposal, he affirms the sanctity of white marriage, leaving the possibility of resistance generated in the story as unfulfilled as the performance itself.

28 April 2000

Lucy is again discussing Conquergood's ethical stances in relation to the other, calling upon people to explain the positions and why Conquergood finds them problematic. Eventually, she arrives at what Conquergood calls the "Skeptic's Cop-out," an unethical positioning of the self in relation to the other in performance. In this position, the performer distances himself/herself while arguing that there is too much difference between the two cultures, resulting in a refusal to engage. Lucy, trying to generate conversation, admits that there are cultural others she can't engage, noting that she "can't do the KKK. I have to distance from them and I can't, for better or worse, engage them."

Tom immediately nods. "Uh huh," he utters.

Lucy continues, "Why might one what to engage them?"

Lakeeshia raises her hand. "You might find you agree." Her comment barely ends before Tom notes, "You may want to just find out what they are thinking." Saul, a nontraditional white-appearing man with long brown hair streaked with gray, remarks that "if you don't engage them, you can't change them." I write down these comments, wondering where the conversation is going. My pencil scribbles out *Lakeeshia*, *Tom*, then *Saul*, putting their words on the page, recording the data, laying the groundwork for what is to come.

Thus far, every "Performing Cultures" class I have taught and observed encounters some kind of extended conversation about the Ku Klux Klan. I find this move interesting because it allows white folks to talk about racism, to talk about the dangers of whiteness, in some kind of distant manner. White students often talk about the actions of the KKK—the things they do, the things they say—with great contempt, yet always use code words like "those people" or mark their voices in some way as to suggest that it is not they. *I heard on the news that the KKK was marching in Washington DC. Yea, haw! Those people are so stupid …* I have grown used to this distancing move. It seems to accomplish two things. First, it locates a discourse of racial hatred as outside themselves—as not-they. In this way, I can talk about racism and never fear that I might be seen as part of the problem. This individualizing move that separates the good, innocent white person from racism locates racism only in intention, and since one never intends harm, one is off the hook for racist actions. Second, the KKK as a site of public bashing also protects whiteness through the citation of extremism. This is to say, whiteness never gets seen as an ideology that runs through everything we do and say, but rather is located in those tiny moments.

Tom raises his hand. "This one time, I was in Saint Vernon. I was in this Denny's and, uh, well, you know that Barton is the KKK base in the southern part of this state, right? Oh, yeah, sorry to those who are from Barton." Tom smiles, looking around the room. "Barton is a hole in the wall, not that Saint Vernon isn't a toilet." He shakes his head and then continues: "So anyway, I was with my brother and we were going to get Van Halen tickets and we went to this Denny's first. We were sitting close to the door and they came in with their black outfits and those crosses and all, that's how we knew who they were. That and they looked like assholes. Anyway, I was wearing my Jim Morrison shirt and they picked us to talk to. They called us faggots cause we had long hair and then they spit on the table. Luckily not on our food though."

Lucy's face grows grave and asks, "Were they served?"

Tom nods. "Yeah, they sat in the back and a friend of mine had to serve them. He said they were bad tippers. They left him like three pennies pushed into their mashed potatoes. That's worse than not getting a tip!" My hand is quickly trying to get down the story Tom tells; the sweat from my hand makes the plastic pencil occasionally slip. I grow both troubled and excited by the details of the story, this story by this very pale, thin young man who has often noted his relationship with his girlfriend. I grow troubled and excited to watch as he narrates this story, interested in the identities he constructs for us: heterosexual but the victim of homophobia, white but the victim of the KKK. He is the target and subject of KKK discourse, but can tell it in a way that still allows him to discuss the quality of their tip. My pen continues writing. There is so much here. I begin to underline key words in the passage I just copied down: Jim Morrison shirt, KKK base, looked like assholes, not on our food though, bad tippers, Van Halen tickets, faggots.

My writing stops when I hear Nate add to the story. "I once got this card at a concert from a guy with a swastika tattoo. The card said, 'This is a social call, the next one is business.'" Nate sits back in his seat, looking outward toward the rest of the class. I sigh, noting on my tablet the double meaning of this card. Nate's white-appearing body might just be the ground from which this man was recruiting, calling upon Nate as a possible ally. Or, perhaps Nate is someone to be feared, although given what I know about him he is not someone the KKK would necessarily want silenced. I am curious about this tale—what does it do, how does it help construct Nate's identity? How does it construct the antiracist white guy that is also the victim? Further, how does it make nonwhite folks feel to hear these stories about the KKK and their white victims? I want to doubt Nate, question the truthfulness of what he said. As I finish writing down Nate's comment, Tom trumps him: "Well, I once saw a card that said 'nigger-killing license.'"

"So where would you put these folks on this map?" asks Lucy, pointing to the Conquergood material on the board to bring them back to the class conversation.

"In Barton," Tom says, stirring some laughter.

Lucy sighs, "On Conquergood?"

"Oh," says Tom, smiling.

9 May 2000

As I walk down the hallway at 7:30 in the morning on this final exam day, I see students entering the room carrying large baskets of props. By the time of the third and final performance, the students have usually upped the ante on the number of props. I see blankets, lamps, books, costumes, and dishes being carried to various corners of the room in preparation for the group performances. The first group is already set up. This group includes Lakeeshia, Ken, Frieda, Tonya, Emmitt, and several others. The performance starts about ten minutes into the class period with Ken telling us that there will be some cussing, since they are striving to show us "reality." A bright strobe light swirls and loud dance music booms from a small radio off stage right. Ken enters, walks up to a makeshift bar, and orders a beer. His friend Emmitt tags along talking about looking for girls. On the opposite side of the room, Lakeeshia and Tonya dance to the music. Lakeeshia, straining to be heard over the music, says, "I'm looking for my knight in shining armor tonight!" They giggle as Ken approaches, clearly looking at Lakeeshia. He reaches up, patting the top of his red hair, as he enters the lighted area surrounding the two dancing women. "Do you want to dance?" he asks. "Yeah!" returns Tonya, giving Ken a looking over, a broad smile on her face. "No, not you." He pushes past her and faces Lakeeshia. "Hey sweet chocolate! I want to get some sweet brown sugar lovin'."

I cough, almost choking on the coffee I brought with me. I blink. Hard. I look at them as the performance continues in the typical way one might predict a piece on interracial dating to go. They meet, they struggle with difficult friends and family, they love, they marry, they prepare for a child. I hear Tonya commenting on the relationship: "It's about time someone looked past race." The performance continues; I take notes amazed every time Ken calls Lakeeshia his "sweet, sweet chocolate." I bite my lip to keep commentary to myself. Suddenly, the lights go out, and voices that surround us yell out "Coon! Nigger-lover! Spade! Half-breed! KKK!" The voices twist and turn around me and I grow a bit uncomfortable. With three loud cracks, the voices stop. Silence. Then the lights return. Ken is lying on the table, his hands crossed on his chest. A voice begins, "We are gathered here today to say goodbye to Ken. His life was taken in an act of pure hatred."

I sit, looking at them finish the performance. An ache grows in my gut as I watch Ken lying there on the table, the "victim" of the KKK and their violence. I watch them honor him. And I think. I think about what it means to again make the white guy the martyr. I think about what it means to have the white guy enter the "jungle" only to be killed, to be disciplined for the crossing. I think about what it means to have Ken be the honorable white guy so clearly removed from the racism that led to his death. I think about what it means for "Sweet Chocolate," the widow with child, to be left. It all seems so wrong. It all seems so easy. It all seems

so very easy. I close my eyes on the final line, knowing
that this, to these students, is an antiracist performance. "Weep not for Ken. He rests now in the bosom of
Jesus. Will you?" This is all so easy. And it's only the
first performance of the morning. I take a sip of coffee, draw a line under my notes, and await the next
scene.

I don't think I am a bad person. I say that for the need to both articulate it on paper, to reassure myself of my self-worth, and reclaim my ethnographic enterprise. I believe the work I do is important. I believe that it has the potential to instigate change. I believe that it contains a kernel of hope, a faith that if one closely examines the reproductive nature of power through whiteness, we might be able to imagine a world in which I, as a white person, do less damage to others. I feel it is my moral responsibility to do this work.

As a white, middle-class, heterosexual, able-bodied man in the world today, I have three possible positions to take in relation to racism—one ignoring it and the other two engaging it. First, I could choose to ignore it, banking on my own privilege to protect me from accountability for what I do. Thus, this position ignores the power of whiteness, allowing the machine to continue to work its violence. Second, I could choose to engage racism, by speaking about nonwhite others. Certainly, this kind of work has been done. The white ethnographer enters the wilderness to find out how the savages feel, to speak only for the other, ignoring the self and how whiteness influences what one hears and how one reports. The third option is to write about whiteness, to engage it from my own location, to study those similar to me, to dissect how whiteness influences myself and others. I could dissect how whiteness is continually re-created by white subjects—to see how white subjects are constituted through the acts of whiteness in interaction.

The only option that I feel is ethical as a white person in the world is to engage it on the local level. To spend my critical time and energy analyzing whiteness is to say, "Yes, there is racism. Yes, I benefit from it. Yes, I will do something about it by trying to interrupt it." It is an ethical position that does not deny scholars of color who preceded my voice, but adds my critical voice in harmony with those voices—to attempt to speak a language that moves people constituted in whiteness from a place of ignorance to a place where people question themselves, their world. This is my ethical responsibility.

Yet, this is not to elide the very real problematic nature of my own position within this research, the fact that I am a white researcher counting on racism for my own material benefit. I will cash in on racism in more ways than most white folks who rely on the mechanisms of privilege to get jobs and access to education, for I will be actually building my career on it. I have written class papers and received praise thanks to racism. I have taken scholarship to conferences based on whiteness and racism. I have received an award based on this work. I have published it. I will look for jobs as a young white academic working on whiteness. This work certainly helped me attain the job I currently hold. This is privilege. This is banking on racism. And this is the other side of my work on whiteness. Yes, I believe that what I do is important and can change people's understandings of race and whiteness, but it does so in ways that continue to grant me power. It is a tension I feel in my body as I try to find peace with my work. It is a tension that I am uncertain how to resolve. Perhaps this is a productive struggle. Perhaps I narrate it only to make myself feel better, to make myself believe that I really am not a bad person—to justify what I do.

Did it work?

Note

[1] Many of the in-class instances discussed here, as well as the in-class performances, are also discussed in chapters 3 and 4. I am repeating them here in an effort to capture the immediacy of the moment.

Epilogue

Performative Possibilities

When I finish writing something, I like to clean my room. Ever since I got my first academic job, I have written in my school office. I write in this little room at the end of West Hall. I like this room, with its institutional brown walls and carpet, my toys scattered across book-filled shelves, and the lamps casting shadows as they deny the fluorescent bulbs their flicker. When I finish writing something, my ritual is to clean. I begin by making stacks of books, files, articles, old drafts, and old paper destined for the trash. I then work through each pile until the room is cleared, the desk free from any evidence of the project that was just completed. This is my ritual.

Well, it is now "the end" and as I try to draw this project to a close, I find that I can't clear up the mess in my office yet. It is still there, piles of drafts covered in orange sticky-notes, disks filled with various versions of the same bits of text, and books laid out to various pages, each of which contains some vitally important quotation. The room looks used. It looks tired. It looks dirty. I suppose most scholars have had rooms like this one, full of matter out of place, out of order, exposed.

For me, I see this room as a place of uncompleted lines of thought. Over by the window, in a small folder, is an idea I had for chapter 3. I think the earlier (longer) drafts of chapter 2 are at the bottom of a stack of student papers. Scattered around me are the places I went, but did not end up writing. Buried in this messiness are the stories I didn't tell, the names I never used, the performances I didn't talk about. Like any writing, there are moments that matter but never get told. There are places to go still in these pages, places yet to be fully seen.

*****

Drawing something to a satisfying end has never been my strong suit. Often in my own reading of others' work, I get to the conclusion and see their recommendations and wonder if they even read their own book. I ask myself, "Do you even see how the careful work you did in this analysis is undermined by your easy ending?" I once read a very exciting book on whiteness and education in which the author ended the analysis by arguing for more diversity training in our teacher preparation programs. I sat bewildered, confused. The complexities of the analysis did not support the easy end; rather, it seemed the analysis actually worked to say that such "training" programs only work on the level of surface treatments and ignore the larger systemic issues involved in race, power, and education. It was a disappointing end that I vowed to not repeat when given the opportunity. Thus, this is not a conclusion, not a list of recommendations imparted by the researcher as he aims for his final page. What I want to mark here is the implications this work has had for me as a teacher and researcher of communication, pedagogy, and culture. In a sense, how has this work affected me?

First, I have tried to take seriously the fundamental implication of this work: whiteness and racial power are constituted through the repeated and mundane communicative acts that carefully work to sediment and reify our understanding of race and difference. This has had a great influence on my everyday communication, including the way I have written this book. For instance, my use of "white-appearing" is to draw attention to the implications of naming—to say, "watch as I signal this language choice." These kinds of changes and monitoring of my own writing and daily talk have affected my teaching as well. In my large lecture course, I now include a lecture on popular culture and communication in which I ask my students to consider the ways the images in the films work to create rhetorical messages, how they construct gender, race, and sexuality through the depictions presented. We look at the films very much like I examine the performances detailed in this book, asking what the choices of language and style do for/to us as audience members. It is to work toward developing a critical literacy (Fassett and Warren; hooks, *Outlaw*), a way of seeing, reading, and theorizing the performances we see. My hope is that these kinds of skills build toward a way of seeing everyday communication. Can students read their everyday lives in ways that are self-reflexive and critical? Can they deconstruct the communicative messages they encounter and ask questions that truly radicalize their/our everyday understandings? This is the first major lesson I learn from this project.

Second, I have created new courses that are specifically aimed at creating space for the kinds of conversations I have modeled in these pages. On the undergraduate and graduate level, I have created courses entitled "Communication, Race, and Power." These courses have had a central focus of uncovering how racial identities and hierarchies have been (and are being) constituted in communication. I have been amazed at the complexity of our conversations in these classes and at the students' ability to not only critically engage social issues of race and power, but to note how communication makes those very ideas possible. When given the chance, our students are able to read their lives (and those around them) performatively. I began this book by noting that I wanted to develop a way of seeing whiteness in production. What I have found through my classroom practice is that students *can* do this—they can theorize about race and power in ways that go to the roots of racial hierarchy. And further, when they do, it is impressive.

Finally, this research project has reminded me of the power of performance. The "Performing Cultures" course in which this study took place made possible these findings—it was the mode of performance as pedagogy that allowed me a peek at the machinery of whiteness. Recently, a friend read my writing and asked if this course was "hell," noting that if I found so many things wrong with this course and the students' performances, then perhaps we should get rid of the course altogether. My response remains clear: The course is necessary precisely because of the potential of performance as a way of knowing. Rather than imagine this course as a site of racial violence, I would argue that this course is a model for engaging in critical antiracist work. The fact that ideals of racism and white supremacy persist in this class demonstrates how pervasive whiteness really is in our (and our students') consciousness. Therefore, if we can combine the magic of performance with the critical insight gained by this performative way of seeing human action, then we might find hope. My own efforts to put these two pedagogical goals together resulted in a series of workshops on whiteness that specifically tries to combine the power of performative analysis with the medium of the lived body. Workshop participants enter the realm of performance to learn about whiteness and cultural power. When I did this work in my summer course, students were able to take newly honed critical reading skills and performative ways of thinking into the body, creating problem-posing images/performances that challenged and complicated our sedimented understandings. In one particular performance, students created a tug-of-war in which a student's body became the rope between two opposing sides: antiracist desires and the seduction of privilege. In the end, the image created a powerful conversation of resistance and cultural possibility.

As I signal a close, I turn to three recent experiences in my classrooms—classrooms that were specifically designed to work through the three tenets described above, hopefully fostering a critical space where students investigated the performativity of whiteness and asked questions about performative possibilities. First, Chad was a young, nineteen-year-old white-appearing student in one of my introductory communication courses. During one class period, I opted to introduce the class to cultural communication through Peggy

McIntosh's essay "White Privilege and Male Privilege." During the discussion, I had many students fighting the context, McIntosh's central claims, and her personalized voice. This kind of reaction is not new; in fact, by now it has become expected. But Chad was somehow different. We went back and forth, challenging and responding to each other. As Chad continued to argue his points, his voice grew louder and louder, his pale cheeks flushed with red. I knew we had taken too much class time here, that I was ignoring my other students, that Chad may not ever see McIntosh's point, but for some reason I continued, allowing the other students to witness this moment. Every point Chad put out, I took away. Every point I put out, Chad denied. He was doing a good job of holding the line on individualization and meritocracy, staying within this conservative logic that we are, as individuals, socially equal.

Finally, I asked Chad why he was so adamant that his position was the only way to see it, the only position to take. I asked him why he couldn't give McIntosh the same ability to articulate her experience as he was asking the class for his own voice. I asked him what was the real reason he couldn't hear her point. In the moments of silence between my voice and his own, I felt the weight of what I had asked him. He looked up at me (were those tears in his eyes, cracks in his voice?) and said, "Because I don't want to live in the world you are saying I live in. I don't want to know that I participate in the violence you have described. I can't do what you are asking of me." Chad remained silent for the remainder of the class hour, but as he left he gave me a look. It wasn't contempt or anger. Not sadness or regret. It looked to me like relief, like he had been thirsty and had just been given water. He looked calm.

I haven't seen Chad in years and do not know how he stories that class event. Perhaps his story is about an impossible instructor who verbally assaulted him. Perhaps he hates me. But for a moment, I felt that he was able to see the mechanisms of whiteness at play in his life. I felt that he was able, even if only for a moment, to see that his holding onto white privilege was about pleasure and comfort—that it was more than the radical individual making individual choices. In the moment he said that he couldn't live in the world I'd created in that classroom, he must have seen, known, or at least imagined that a world, equally created and maintained, existed outside that classroom. And that realization, those ripples in the waters of whiteness's strength, must have been something for him. I hope that relief I saw created a desire to know more. Perhaps it did. Perhaps the performative process, so powerful at seduction, brought him back to blindness. But for a moment, I think he saw something more.

A similar experience occurred with Andre, a young African American student in my senior-level "Communication, Race, and Power" course. He wrote a powerful poetic essay in response to the following prompt: "What have you learned about communication, race, and power?" His essay began with an allusion to *The Matrix*, a film in which a central figure offers Neo (our hero) two pills, each with its own consequences. If he takes the blue pill, he wakes up in bed and he will never know the truth. If he takes the red pill, he wakes up and realizes that the world he knows is a lie. Neo takes the red pill. Andre's opening set the stage for a dramatic and engaging essay about how this course, my course, had opened his eyes to a set of lies. Like Chad, Andre had fought to keep his own illusions, his own blindness, in place. To really engage this material was to question his white friends, his white teachers, his white government, his white life—after this class, he had to live in the world revealed. The pain of his narrative as he described how the mechanisms of whiteness had seduced him is a reminder that whiteness's pull is beyond the body, beyond the essentialized images often presented. It is to open up experience and ask the question: If this is a performative process, how can we see how each of us participates to varying degrees, with varying rewards and punishments, to maintain the machine?

Andre's response *is* complicated. Andre put himself on the line, offering his own experience and his life for us to see just how deep the system's roots truly are. His words, crafted and specific, reminded me of why I conducted this study, why I was drawn to the lives and stories of others. For in those stories, we see not only how power gets instituted, but how power can be, potentially, challenged. It would be difficult for anyone to hear Andre's poetic narrative and deny him that experience—to deny, if we really listen to the way Chad's voice cracked with pain and anger, that we too have been changed.

Finally, I turn to a whiteness workshop I conducted in a recent education and culture class. I began by breaking students into groups and asked them to create lists of those issues in the course that still plagued them. They did, and together we compiled a master list on the board. Then I grouped those issues into five main categories. Based on those, I divided the twenty students into five groups and asked each group to create a performance that tried to embody the issue—to pose a problem derived from that particular point of interest. For instance, one group struggled with trying to find a balance in their own personal self-negotiation between the power of privilege and the desire to bring about change. A white woman, arms outstretched between two other people, became the rope in a tug-of-war. On the left was Howard, a black man, who spoke of resistance: "You can do it. Keep going!" Sophia, a white woman, on the right, was the embodiment of privilege: "Why bother? It's too hard." This continued for a minute until the woman broke out of the tug-of-war, asking each member of the class audience for help, ending up back as the rope between Howard and Sophia. She ends the performance by looking up and, again, asking for help.

After the performance, students talked about how it felt to be in that situation: how it felt to be asked for help and not providing it, how it felt to be the rope—to feel the pull of these opposing forces; how it felt to see that struggle embodied. That day changed the tenor of the class as people began to see whiteness in their own actions, their own bodies. Each performance brought to the body the power of whiteness and made it tangible. To see themselves meant risking privilege. It meant upsetting the fragile racial center of power on which they relied, reflecting and critiquing their own bodily complicity with racism (Warren, "Performative Pedagogy").

In this final example, I feel the connections between performance, whiteness, and possibility. This example, this brief moment, of performance became the vehicle for hope, for change. The moment was so vivid in that room—I remember Howard and Sophia pulling, tugging on the white woman in the middle, whispering their influence into her ears. I remember her looking so confused, so tired. I recall her during the debriefing period after the performance ended: "I wasn't expecting to feel so conflicted in the performance—I was expecting it to be pretend, to be like I was in a play. Yet, when I was being pulled by Howard and Sophia, it really felt authentic—it felt real. And it was hard to keep moving through the performance because I felt that if I made a mistake and did not anticipate the tug, they could really hurt me. It was just a few minutes, but I am tired as a result." I smile now, knowing this feeling in my own body—knowing that this is precisely the power of performance. It is precisely the power of performance to highlight the tensions of our everyday lives in ways that make us understand the forces at work in our negotiations of race and power.

As I think about this woman now, I somehow know that the next time she is in the presence of a racist comment, a comment made in ignorance or spite against someone of another race, a comment meant to push up whiteness at the expense of others, she will feel those arms on hers—she will feel Howard and Sophia's grip and know that she must negotiate the tensions or risk choosing. Either choice is risky—choosing to rely on privilege with the new knowledge that such choices enact violence will risk her sense of self, her sense of right and wrong. Choosing to resist, to side with Howard, to allow the critical voice to rise within her to mark racism in action, will also be a risk. She will feel the tug and know that it is no longer an easy choice, for ultimately it is Howard at the end of that grip—it is a new friend made in this class that gets implicated in her decisions. She, after this performance, is changed. The moment of bodily engagement means that the machinery, the constructed and regulated mechanisms of whiteness, are now part of her felt knowledge (Warren, "Performative Pedagogy").

The three vectors (developing a critical literacy of possibility, new contexts for dialogue and critique, and the power of performance) I have described here are not solutions. Rather, they each are ways, modes, possibilities for engaging the machinery, the reproductive system of power, of whiteness. Each needs more development, more critical work. This is not a conclusion. Rather, the conclusion remains a performative possibility. It is what we make of it.

*****

I decide, for the time being, to let the piles stay in my little office—to let them just sit there, reminding me of what this project was really all about. This whole project has been about seeing the piles on the floor as a kind of order. To see the matter out of place as a construction. My desire to clean it all up, to erase the residue of the last several years, is a desire to return to some illusion of normalcy. It is a desire to fall back on the privilege of my own comfort at the expense of the voices that "litter" my office—those voices that are telling me to be uncomfortable with the comfortable. I will let the piles stay, for now. I will let them speak to me. And when I do put them away, as I know I eventually will, I will try to remember the lessons they have taught me. I will try not to forget. I will try not to let the blurring tendency of whiteness make these voices fade away, forever erasing themselves as the machine attempts to reseduce me.

Bibliography

Alexander, Bryant K. "Performing Culture in the Classroom: An Instructional (Auto) Ethnography." *Text and Performance Quarterly* 19 (1999): 307–331.

Asante, Molefi Kete. "The Escape into Hyperbole: Communication and Political Correctness." *Journal of Communication* 42.2 (1992): 141–47.

Austin, J. L. *How to Do Things with Words*. 2nd ed. Cambridge, MA: Harvard University Press, 1975.

Bacon, Wallace A. "The Dangerous Shores: A Decade Later." *The Study of Oral Interpretation: Theory and Comment*. Ed. Richard Haas and David A. Williams. Indianapolis: Bobbs-Merrill, 1975, 221–28.

———. "The Dangerous Shores: From Elocution to Interpretation." *The Quarterly Journal of Speech* 46 (1960): 148–52.

———. "The Dangerous Shores: One Last Time." *Text and Performance Quarterly* 16 (1996): 356–58.

Beaty, Jerome, and J. Paul Hunter, eds. *New Worlds of Literature: Writings from America's Many Cultures*. 2nd ed. New York: W. W. Norton and Company, 1994.

Bérubé, Allan, with Florence Bérubé. "Sunset Trailer Park." *White Trash: Race and Class in America*. Ed. Matt Wray and Annalee Newitz. New York: Routledge, 1997, 15–39.

Bohman, James. *New Philosophy of Social Science*. Cambridge: Massachusetts Institute of Technology Press, 1991.

Butler, Judith. *Bodies That Matter: On the Discursive Limits of 'Sex.'* New York: Routledge, 1993.

———. *Excitable Speech: A Politics of the Performative*. New York: Routledge, 1997.

———. "Performative Acts and Gender Constitution: An Essay in Phenomenology and Feminist Theory." *Performing Feminisms: Feminist Critical Theory and Theatre*. Ed. Sue Ellen Case. Baltimore: Johns Hopkins University Press, 1990, 270–82.

Carey, James W. "Political Correctness and Cultural Studies." *Journal of Communication* 42.2 (1992): 56–72.

Carger, Chris Liska. *Of Borders and Dreams: A Mexican American Experience of Urban Education*. New York: Teachers College Press, 1996.

Carter, Robert C. "Is White a Race? Expressions of White Racial Identity." *Off White: Readings on Race, Power, and Society*. Ed. Michelle Fine, Lois Weis, Linda C. Powell, and L. Mun Wong. New York: Routledge, 1997, 198–209.

Chambers, Ross. "The Unexamined." *Whiteness: A Critical Reader*. Ed. Mike Hill. New York: NYU Press, 1997, 187–203.

Clifford, James. "Introduction: Partial Truths." *Writing Culture: The Poetics and Politics of Ethnography*. Ed. James Clifford and George E. Marcus. Berkeley and Los Angeles: University of California Press, 1986, 1–26.

——. "On Ethnographic Allegory." *Writing Culture: The Poetics and Politics of Ethnography*. Ed. James Clifford and George E. Marcus. Berkeley and Los Angeles: University of California Press, 1986, 98–121.

Clifford, James, and George E. Marcus, eds. *Writing Culture: The Poetics and Politics of Ethnography*. Berkeley and Los Angeles: University of California Press, 1986.

Conquergood, Dwight. "Health Theatre in a Hmong Refugee Camp: Performance, Communication, and Culture." *The Drama Review* 3 (1988): 174–208.

——. "Homeboys and Hoods: Gang Communication and Cultural Space." *Group Communication in Context: Studies of Natural Groups*. Ed. Lawrence R. Frey. Hillsdale, NJ: Lawrence Erlbaum Assoc., 1994, 23–55.

——. "Performing as a Moral Act: Ethical Dimensions of the Ethnography of Performance." *Literature in Performance* 5.2 (1985): 1–13.

——. "Rethinking Ethnography: Towards a Critical Cultural Politics." *Communication Monographs* 58 (1991): 179–94.

Corey, Frederick C. "Performing Sexualities in an Irish Pub." *Text and Performance Quarterly* 16 (1996): 146–60.

Crenshaw, Carrie. "Resisting Whiteness' Rhetorical Silence." *Western Journal of Communication* 61 (1997): 253–78.

Daniels, Jessie. *White Lies: Race, Class, Gender, and Sexuality in White Supremacy Discourse*. New York: Routledge, 1997.

Delpit, Lisa. *Other People's Children: Cultural Conflicts in the Classroom*. New York: The New Press, 1995.

Diamond, Elin. Introduction. *Performance and Cultural Politics*. Ed. Elin Diamond. NY: Routledge, 1996, 1–12.

Douglas, Mary. *Purity and Danger: An Analysis of the Concepts of Pollution and Taboo*. New York: Ark Paperbooks, 1966.

Dunbar, Roxanne A. "Bloody Footprints: Reflections on Growing Up Poor White." *White Trash: Race and Class in America*. Ed. Matt Wray and Annalee Newitz. New York: Routledge, 1997, 73–86.

Dyer, Richard. "White." *Screen* 29.4 (1988): 44–64.

——. *White*. London: Routledge, 1997.

Ellsworth, Elizabeth. "Double Binds of Whiteness." *Off White: Readings on Race, Power, and Society*. Ed. Michelle Fine, Lois Weis, Linda C. Powell, and L. Mun Wong. New York: Routledge, 1997, 259–69.

Emerson, Robert M., Rachel I. Fretz, and Linda L. Shaw. *Writing Ethnographic Fieldnotes*. Chicago: University of Chicago Press, 1995.

Fanon, Frantz. *Black Skin, White Masks*. Trans. Charles Lam Markmann. New York: Grove Press, 1967.

Fassett, Deanna L., and John T. Warren. "A Teacher Wrote This Movie: Challenging the Myths of *187*." *Multicultural Education* 7 (1999): 31–33.

Fine, Michelle. *Framing Dropouts: Notes on the Politics of Urban Public High School*. Albany: SUNY Press, 1991.

Fiske, John. "For Cultural Interpretation: A Study of the Culture of Homelessness." *Critical Studies in Mass Communication* 8 (1991): 455–74.

——. "Writing Ethnographies: Contribution to a Dialogue." *Quarterly Journal of Speech* 77 (1991): 330–35.

Fordham, Signithia. "'Those Loud Black Girls': (Black) Women, Silence, and Gender 'Passing' in the Academy." *Beyond Black and White: New Faces and Voices in U.S. Schools*. Ed. Maxine Seller and Lois Weis. Albany: SUNY Press, 1997, 81–111.

Foucault, Michel. *Discipline and Punish: The Birth of the Prison*. Trans. Alan Sheridan. New York: Vintage, 1977.

——. *Power/Knowledge: Selected Interviews and Other Writings*. Ed. Colin Gordon. New York: Pantheon Books, 1980.

Frankenberg, Ruth. *White Women, Race Matters: The Social Construction of Whiteness*. Minneapolis: University of Minnesota Press, 1993.

Fuoss, Kirk W. "Lynching Performances, Theatres of Violence." *Text and Performance Quarterly* 19 (1999): 1–37.

Geertz, Clifford. *The Interpretation of Cultures: Selected Essays*. New York: Basic Books, 1973.

——. *Local Knowledge: Further Essays in Interpretative Anthropology*. New York: Basic Books, 1983.

——. *Works and Lives: The Anthropologist as Author*. Stanford: Stanford University Press, 1988.

Gingrich-Philbrook, Craig. "Refreshment." *Text and Performance Quarterly* 17 (1997): 352–60.

Giroux, Henry A. "Rewriting the Discourse of Racial Identity: Towards a Pedagogy and Politics of Whiteness." *Harvard Educational Review* 67 (1997): 285–320.

Goodall, H. L. *Writing the New Ethnography*. Walnut Creek, CA: AltaMira Press, 2000.

Gould, Timothy. "The Unhappy Performative." *Performance and Performativity*. Bloomington: Indiana University Press, 1995, 19–44.

Hammersley, Martyn, and Paul Atkinson. *Ethnography: Principles in Practice*. 2nd ed. New York: Routledge, 1995.

Hartigan, John, Jr. "Locating White Detroit." *Displacing Whiteness: Essays in Social and Cultural Criticism*. Ed. Ruth Frankenberg. Durham, NC: Duke University Press, 1997, 180–213.

——. "Name Calling: Objectifying 'Poor Whites' and 'White Trash' in Detroit." *White Trash: Race and Class in America*. Ed. Matt Wray and Annalee Newitz. New York: Routledge, 1997, 42–56.

——. *Racial Situations: Class Predicaments of Whiteness in Detroit*. Princeton, NJ: Princeton University Press, 1999.

Helms, Janet. *Black and White Racial Identity: Theory, Research, and Practice*. Westport, CT: Greenwood Press, 1990.

hooks, bell. *Killing Rage: Ending Racism*. New York: Owl Books, 1995.

——. *Outlaw Culture: Resisting Representations*. New York: Routledge, 1994.

——. *Teaching to Transgress: Education as the Practice of Freedom*. New York: Routledge, 1994.

——. *Yearning: Race, Gender, and Cultural Politics*. Boston: South End Press, 1990.

Hytten, Kathy, and John T. Warren. "Engaging Whiteness: How Racial Power Gets Reified in Education." *International Journal of Qualitative Studies in Education* 16 (2003): 65–89.

Jackson, Ronald L., II. "White Space, White Privilege: Mapping Discursive Inquiry into the Self." *Quarterly Journal of Speech* 85 (1999): 38–54.

Jackson, Shannon. "Representing Rape: Model Mugging's Discursive and Embodied Perform-
    ances." *The Drama Review* 37 (1993): 110–41.
———. "White Privilege and Pedagogy: Nadine Gordimer in Performance." *Theatre Topics* 7
    (1997): 117–38.
Johnson, Parker C. "Reflections on Critical White(ness) Studies." *Whiteness: The Communication of
    Social Identity*. Ed. Thomas K. Nakayama and Judith Martin. Thousand Oaks, CA: Sage, 1999,
    1–9.
Keating, AnnLouise. "Interrogating 'Whiteness,' (De)Constructing 'Race.'" *College English* 57
    (1995): 901–18.
Kohl, Herbert. *"I Won't Learn from You": And Other Creative Thoughts on Creative Maladjustments*. New
    York: The New Press, 1994.
Lakoff, George, and Mark Johnson. *Metaphors We Live By*. Chicago: University of Chicago Press,
    1980.
Langsdorf, Lenore. "'I Like to Watch': Analyzing a Participation-and-Denial Phenomenon." *Hu-
    man Studies* 17 (1994): 81–108.
Leder, Drew. *The Absent Body*. Chicago: University of Chicago Press, 1990.
Lindlof, Thomas R. *Qualitative Communication Research Methods*. Thousand Oaks, CA: Sage, 1995.
Lofland, John, and Lyn H. Lofland. *Analyzing Social Settings: A Guide to Qualitative Observation and
    Analysis*. 3rd ed. Belmont, CA: Wadsworth, 1995.
Lorde, Audre. *Sister Outsider*. Freedom, CA: The Crossing Press, 1984.
Madison, Kelly J. "Legitimization Crisis and Containment: The 'Anti-Racist-White-Hero' Film."
    Critical Studies in Mass Communication 16 (1999): 399–416.
Maher, Frances, and Mary Kay Thompson Tetreault. " 'They got the Paradigm and Painted it
    White': Whiteness and Pedagogies of Positionality." *White Reign: Deploying Whiteness in Amer-
    ica*. Ed. Joe L. Kincheloe, Shirley R. Steinberg, Nelson M. Rodriguez, and Ronald E. Chen-
    nault. New York: St. Martin's Press, 1998, 137–158.
Martin, Judith N., Robert L. Krizek, Thomas K. Nakayama, and Lisa Bradford. "Exploring
    Whiteness: A Study of Self-Labels for White Americans." *Communication Quarterly* 44 (1996):
    125–44.
Martin, Judith N., and Thomas K. Nakayama. *Intercultural Communication in Contexts*. 2nd ed. Moun-
    tain View, CA: Mayfield Publishing Co., 2000.
McCarthy, Cameron, and Warren Crichlow, eds. *Race, Identity, and Representation in Education*. New
    York: Routledge, 1993.
McIntosh, Peggy. "White Privilege and Male Privilege: A Personal Account of Coming to See
    Correspondences through Work in Women's Studies." Working Paper No. 189. Wellesley
    College Center for Research on Women, 1988.
McIntyre, Alice. *Making Meaning of Whiteness: Exploring Racial Identity with White Teachers*. Albany:
    SUNY Press, 1997.
McKerrow, Raymie E. "Critical Rhetoric: Theory and Praxis." *Communication Monographs* 56
    (1989): 91–111.
McLaren, Peter. "Decentering Whiteness." *Multicultural Education* 5 (1997): 4–11.
———. *Schooling as a Ritual Performance: Toward a Political Economy of Educational Systems and Gestures*.
    2nd ed. New York: Routledge, 1993.

——. "Unthinking Whiteness, Rethinking Democracy: Critical Citizenship in Gringolandia." *Becoming and Unbecoming White: Owning and Disowning a Racial Identity.* Ed. Christine Clark and James O'Donnell. Westport, CT: Bergin and Garvey, 1999, 10–55.

McQuillan, Patrick James. *Educational Opportunity in an Urban American High School: A Cultural Analysis.* Albany: SUNY Press, 1998.

Miller, Jackson B. "'Indians,' 'Braves,' and 'Redskins': A Performative Struggle for Control of an Image." *Quarterly Journal of Speech* 82 (1999): 188–202.

Montag, Warren. "The Universalization of Whiteness: Racism and Enlightenment." *Whiteness: A Critical Reader.* Ed. Mike Hill. New York: NYU Press, 1997, 281–93.

Moon, Dreama. "White Enculturation and Bourgeois Ideology: The Discursive Production of 'Good (White) Girls.'" *Whiteness: The Communication of Social Identity.* Ed. Thomas K. Nakayama and Judith Martin. Thousand Oaks, CA: Sage, 1999, 177–97.

Morrison, Toni. *Playing in the Dark: Whiteness and the Literary Imagination.* New York: Vintage, 1992.

Nakayama, Thomas K., and Robert L. Krizek. "Whiteness: A Strategic Rhetoric." *Quarterly Journal of Speech* 81 (1995): 291–309.

Orbe, Mark P. "'Remember, It's Always Whites' Ball': Descriptions of African-American Male Communication." *Communication Quarterly* 42 (1994): 287–300.

Pelias, Ronald J. "Performative Writing as Scholarship: An Apology, an Argument, an Anecdote." Paper presented at the National Communication Association convention, New York, NY (November 1998).

——. *Writing Performance: Poetizing the Researcher's Body.* Carbondale: Southern Illinois University Press, 1999.

Phelan, Peggy. *Unmarked: The Politics of Performance.* New York: Routledge, 1993.

Pineau, Elyse Lamm. "*Nursing Mother* and Articulating Absence." *Text and Performance Quarterly* 20 (2000): 1–19.

——. "Teaching is Performance: Reconceptualizing a Problematic Metaphor." *American Educational Research Journal* 31 (1994): 3–25.

Pollock, Della. "Performing Writing." *The Ends of Performance.* Ed. Peggy Phelan and Jill Lane. New York: NYU Press, 1998, 73–103.

Powell, Linda C. "The Achievement (K)not: Whiteness and 'Black Underachievement.'" *Off White: Readings on Race, Power, and Society.* Ed. Michelle Fine, Lois Weis, Linda C. Powell, and L. Mun Wong. New York: Routledge, 1997, 3–12.

Projansky, Sarah, and Kent A. Ono. "Strategic Whiteness as Cinematic Racial Politics." *Whiteness: The Communication of Social Identity.* Ed. Thomas K. Nakayama and Judith Martin. Thousand Oaks, CA: Sage, 1999, 149–74.

Richardson, Troy, and Sofia Villenas. "'Other' Encounters: Dances with Whiteness in Multicultural Education." *Educational Theory* 50 (2000): 255–73.

Rodriguez, Nelson M. "Projects of Whiteness in a Critical Pedagogy." *Dismantling Whiteness: Pedagogy, Politics, and Whiteness.* Ed. Nelson M. Rodriguez and Leila E. Villaverde. New York: Peter Lang, 2000, 1–24.

Rodriguez, Nelson M. and Leila E. Villaverde, eds. *Dismantling White Privilege: Pedagogy, Politics, and Whiteness.* New York: Peter Lang, 2000.

Roediger, David R. "White Looks: Hairy Apes, True Stories, and Limbaugh's Laughs." *Whiteness: A Critical Reader*. Ed. Mike Hill. New York: NYU Press, 1997, 35–46.

Rosaldo, Renato. *Culture and Truth: The Remaking of Social Analysis*. Boston: Beacon Press, 1993.

Ryan, William. *Blaming the Victim*. Rev. ed. New York: Vintage, 1976.

Scheible, Dean. "Faking Identity in Clubland: The Communicative Performance of 'Fake ID.'" *Text and Performance Quarterly* 12 (1992): 160–75.

Scheurich, James Joseph. "Toward a White Discourse on White Racism." *Educational Researcher* 22.8 (1993): 5–16.

Scott, James C. *Domination and the Arts of Resistance: Hidden Transcripts*. New Haven: Yale University Press, 1990.

Sheets, Rosa Hernández, and Etta R. Hollins, eds. *Racial and Ethnic Identity in School Practices: Aspects of Human Development*. Mahwah, NJ: Lawrence Erlbaum, 1999.

Shome, Raka. "Race and Popular Cinema: The Rhetorical Strategies of Whiteness in *City of Joy*." *Communication Quarterly* 44 (1996): 502–18.

———. "Whiteness and the Politics of Location: Postcolonial Reflections." *Whiteness: The Communication of Social Identity*. Ed. Thomas K. Nakayama and Judith Martin. Thousand Oaks, CA: Sage, 1999, 107–28.

Sleeter, Christine E. "How White Teachers Construct Race." *Race, Identity, and Representation in Education*. Ed. Cameron McCarthy and Warren Crichlow. New York: Routledge, 1993, 157–71.

———. *Multicultural Education as Activism*. Albany: SUNY Press, 1996.

Spry, Tami. "Skins: A Daughter's (Re)Construction of Cancer. A Performative Autobiography." *Text and Performance Quarterly* 17 (1997): 361–65.

Staub, Michael E. "The Whitest I: On Reading the Hill-Thomas Transcripts." *Whiteness: A Critical Reader*. Ed. Mike Hill. New York: NYU Press, 1997, 47–62.

Sweeney, Gael. "The King of White Trash Culture: Elvis Presley and the Aesthetics of Excess." *White Trash: Race and Class in America*. Ed. Matt Wray and Annalee Newitz. New York: Routledge, 1997, 249–66.

Tatum, Beverly Daniel. "Teaching White Students about Racism: The Search for White Allies and the Restoration of Hope." *Teachers College Record* 95 (1994): 462–76.

Thomas, Laurence. "Next Life, I'll Be White." *New Worlds of Literature: Writings from America's Many Cultures*. 2nd ed. Ed. Jerome Beaty and J. Paul Hunter. New York: W. W. Norton and Company, 1994, 578–80.

Thompson, Audrey. "Colortalk: Whiteness and *Off White*." *Educational Studies* 30 (1999): 141–60.

Treinen, Kristen P., and John T. Warren. "Anti-Racist Pedagogy in the Basic Course: Teaching Cultural Communication As If Whiteness Matters." *Basic Communication Course Annual* 13 (2001): 46–75.

Trinh T. Minh-ha. "Difference: A Special Third World Women Issue." *Discourse* 8 (1986–87): 11–37.

Valdés, Guadalupe. *Con Respeto: Bridging the Distances Between Culturally Diverse Families and Schools*. New York: Teachers College Press, 1996.

VanMaanen, John. *Tales from the Field: On Writing Ethnography*. Chicago: University of Chicago Press, 1988.

Warren, John T. "Absence for Whom? An Autoethnography of White Subjectivity." *Cultural Studies ←→ Critical Methodologies* 1 (2001): 36–49.

———. "Doing Whiteness: On the Performative Dimensions of Race in the Classroom." *Communication Education* 50 (2001): 91–108.

———. "Performative Pedagogy, At-Risk Students, and the Basic Course: 14 Moments in Search of Possibility." *Basic Communication Course Annual* 15 (2003): 83–116.

———. "Performing Whiteness Differently: Rethinking the Abolitionist Project." *Educational Theory* 51 (2001): 451–66.

———. "The Social Drama of a 'Rice Burner': A (Re)Constitution of Whiteness." *Western Journal of Communication* 65 (2001): 184–205.

———. "Whiteness and Cultural Theory: Perspectives on Research and Education." *The Urban Review* 31 (1999): 185–203.

Warren, John T., and Deanna L. Fassett. "(Re)Constituting Ethnographic Identities." *Qualitative Inquiry* 8 (2002): 575–90.

West, Cornel. *Race Matters*. New York: Vintage, 1993.

Willis, Paul. *Learning to Labour: How Working Class Kids Get Working Class Jobs*. New York: Columbia University Press, 1977.

Wolcott, Harry F. *Writing Up Qualitative Research*. Newbury Park, CA: Sage, 1990.

Wray, Matt. "White Trash Religion." *White Trash: Race and Class in America*. Ed. Matt Wray and Annalee Newitz. New York: Routledge, 1997, 193–210.

Wray, Matt, and Annalee Newtiz, eds. *White Trash: Race and Class in America*. New York: Routledge, 1997.

Index

Critical
Intercultural
Communication
Studies

General Editor, Thomas K. Nakayama

Critical approaches to the study of intercultural communication have arisen at the end of the twentieth century and are poised to flourish in the new millenium. As cultures come into contact— driven by migration, refugees, the internet, wars, media, transnational capitalism, cultural imperialism, and more—critical interrogations of the ways that cultures interact communicatively are needed to understand culture and communication. This series will interrogate—from a critical perspective—the role of communication in intercultural contact, in both domestic and international contexts. This series is open to studies in key areas such as postcolonialism, transnationalism, critical race theory, queer diaspora studies, and critical feminist approaches as they relate to intercultural communication, tuning into the complexities of power relations in intercultural communication. Proposals might focus on various contexts of intercultural communication such as international advertising, popular culture, language policies, hate crimes, ethnic cleansing and ethnic group conflicts, as well as engaging theoretical issues such as hybridity, displacement, multiplicity, identity, orientalism, and materialism. By creating a space for these critical approaches, this series will be at the forefront of this new wave in intercultural communication scholarship. Manuscripts and proposals are welcome that advance this new approach.

For additional information about this series or for the submission of manuscripts, please contact:

Dr. Thomas K. Nakayama
Hugh Downs School of Human Communication
Arizona State University
P.O. Box 871205
Tempe, AZ 85287-1205

To order other books in this series, please contact our Customer Service Department:
(800) 770-LANG (within the U.S.)
(212) 647-7706 (outside the U.S.)
(212) 647-7707 FAX

Or browse online by series:
www.peterlangusa.com